Single Letter Sounds

AF446697

WARNING!
Lots of crazy words!

Author: Matthew Hitch

Co-author: Sunok Moon

Illustrator: Matthew Hitch

Cover Design: Brittany Hitch

Layout Design: Matthew Hitch

Text Design: Matthew Hitch

Image Manager: Matthew Hitch

~~Vain Meglomaniac: Matthew Hitch~~

Credits Editor: Matthew Hitch

Image Manager Manager: S. Moon

Image Manager Manager Control: Absolutely no one

Artistic Arguer: Sunok Moon

Dishwasher: Matthew Hitch
(occasionally Sunok Moon)

Title: Captain Matt's Super Crazy Fun

Kindergarten Phonics 1 Student Book

ISBN 979-11-93590-05-8

First published 2024

Published by Hitch Publishing

info@supercrazyfun.net

This textbook came about as the result of 20 years of trying to make kids enjoy learning English. It is designed around the use of the rhotic R and other characteristics of English pronunciation common in North America. We believe it can be used in other parts of the world as most phonics books can, and we are keen to hear feedback from anyone who tries this.

We want to make clear that the word "crazy" used in the title is in relation to any of the common definitions illustrated below, and does not refer in any way to the meaning "insane."

strange/illogical   **wild**   **unexpected**   **fun**   **unwise**

About the Authors:

Matthew Hitch has taught English in Korea for the better part of 20 years and holds a master's degree in applied linguistics. He clearly does not have a pig nose, and by most accounts is not at all malodorous. He also cuts a dashing figure according to his wife.

Sunok Moon prefers to go by the name Michelle, and is in fact quite scary as reported in the bio on the back of this book. She has a degree in English literature and has taught English in Korea for approximately 3 weeks longer than Matthew, who is writing this and finds it weird to refer to himself in the third person.

Contents

Welcome parents and teachers!

Thank you for considering our book. Phonics books are notoriously boring, so this is the last bastion of publishing where even the tiniest bit of creativity can raise the bar (sorry phonics book publishers, but it's true). With that said, we humbly offer you our content. We have also intentionally challenged convention in a few ways. Much of what we have to say may be used or discarded though, and these books can be used just like any other mainstream phonics book. We hope you will choose to use whatever you please and dispose of the rest.

Please allow us to explain just where our method of teaching phonics may diverge from mainstream approaches, and please do forgive us for sharing information from what is undeniably the most mind-numbingly boring and seemingly useless field of study, linguistics. Most phonics books are not written by scholars in the field of linguistics. They are mostly written by early childhood educators, so perhaps that's the first divergence. We'll start with how we sound out consonants. In linguistic studies it is not uncommon for consonants to be distinguished by using a vowel (usually "ah") on both sides. This means a "V" sounds like "ahvah" and an "F" sounds like "ahfah" and so on. Most phonics books distinguish consonant sounds without such preceding vowel, but they do follow with a vowel in the form of the schwa. This is fine for most consonants, but the ones that are able to be maintained until breath is exhausted can be confusing with a schwa where they end a word. It's mostly ESL students who feel this confusion, but we think it doesn't hurt to teach those consonants without a schwa to native speakers as well, so where "V" sounds like "və" in most phonics books, in our book it is presented as "vvvvvvv" with no schwa. We apply this to all long consonant sounds in our audio files (L,M,N&R are also presented as long with a tiny schwa sound at the end though). If you have read this far, we take our hats off to you. Most would be fast asleep by now.

The next divergence is our use of Magic E. We chose Magic E for the fun potential. The Split Digraphs just can't seem to hold a crowd. Magic E is no longer used in most educational settings for many reasons, but mostly because as a rule it cannot be defined clearly. We do mention that split digraphs are better though, mainly to extend an olive branch to all the teachers we hope will buy our books.

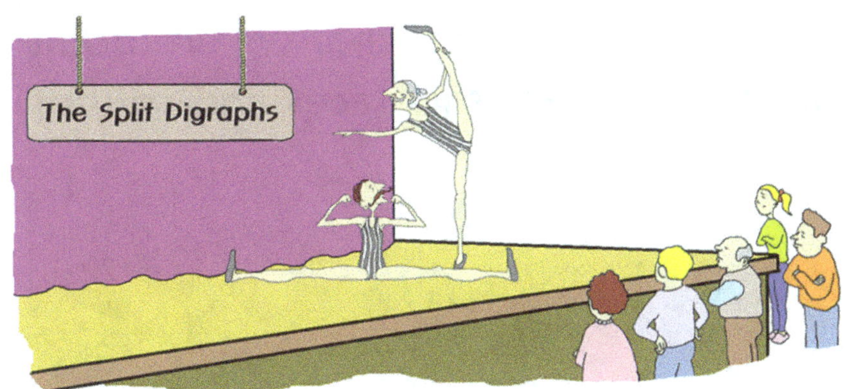

And the final divergence we would like to mention is our choice of words. Our choice of words may seem a bit odd at times throughout the books, but we chose them for their potential for keeping kids engaged over their usefulness. We approach a phonics book as a tool to teach about sounds much more than vocabulary. Poop, vomit, spit, fart, snot, and burp are the most popular with our students. We tried to find a spot for booger, but alas...

Our word choice is also strange in that it includes words that have the long E vowel when teaching split digraphs. Most phonics books glance over the long E vowel. The argument we have heard for this is that it is difficult for the younger students, but we suspect that it's avoided more because it's difficult for authors to find suitable words. We decided to give it a try, and our experience is that the long E words we chose are not that difficult for our students to grasp. Given that English is their second language, we believe native English speaking kids will cope with them just fine. Also you may notice our sight words are not all actually sight words - oops! Anyway, we hope you enjoy our silly books.

Welcome students!

Hello. I am a gorilla. Together we are going to make a lot of very silly faces and sounds!

Hello. I am an elephant. I am a little wide. Some letters are also a little wide. You will see me around them!

Tracks 1-9

Hello. I am a lizard. I am a little thin. Some letters are also a little thin. You will see me around them!

Hello. I am a mole. I like to dig! Some letters also like to dig. You will see me around them!

Hello. I am a pig. I don't care about letters. I just hang around.

I am a fly. I am smelly. You will see me around smelly stuff.

Let's get started...

Welcome Students!   **5**

Listen, point and say 

A B C D E

F G H I J

K L M N O

P Q R S T

U V W X Y

Z z z z z z z z

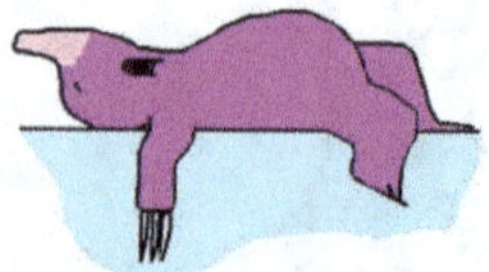

Sing along:

A B C D E F G~
H I J K L M N ~
O P Q..

A B C D E F G ~
H I J K L-M-N-O-P ~
Q R S T U V ~
W X Y & Z

The Alphabet

The Written Alphabet

Writing has rules. If we don't follow them we might seem a bit silly! But then again, it's okay to be a bit silly sometimes, isn't it?

We should write all letters on the line, but small g, j, p, q, and y go under the line a little, like a mole digging a hole!

Vertical lines go down, and horizontal lines go left to right! All circles are are counter-clockwise, except circles connected to the righthand side of a line. Dots and crossing lines are last!

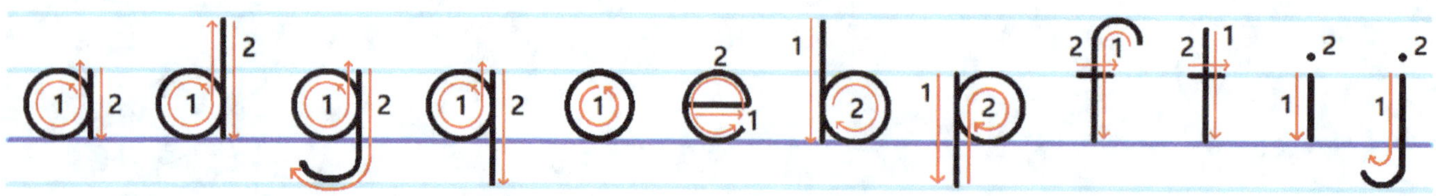

The Alphabet

The typed Alphabet

Typed letters can be a bit confusing. Sometimes there are extra curls or lines missing. We think these three are the most important ones for you to know:

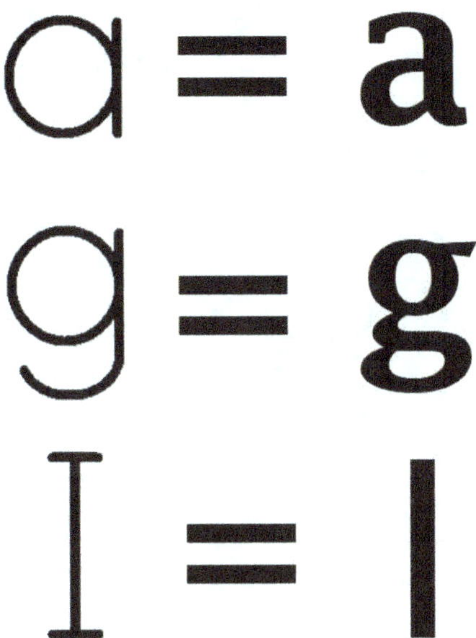

a = **a**

g = **g**

I = l

Your Writing

We don't like to tell people how to write, but we want the best for you, so we show you these writing rules. You can use them if you wish.
Your style can be however you like:

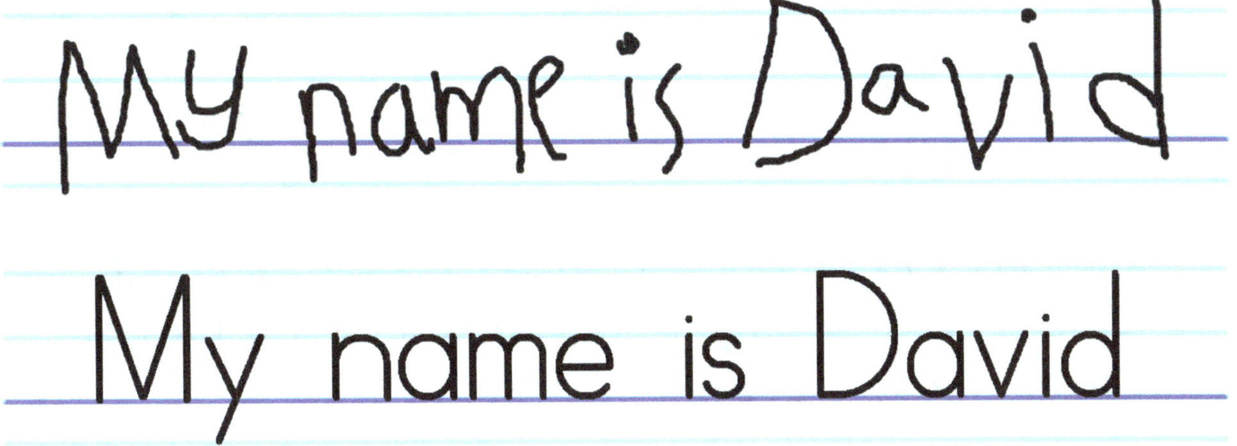

Vowels

Name	Sound

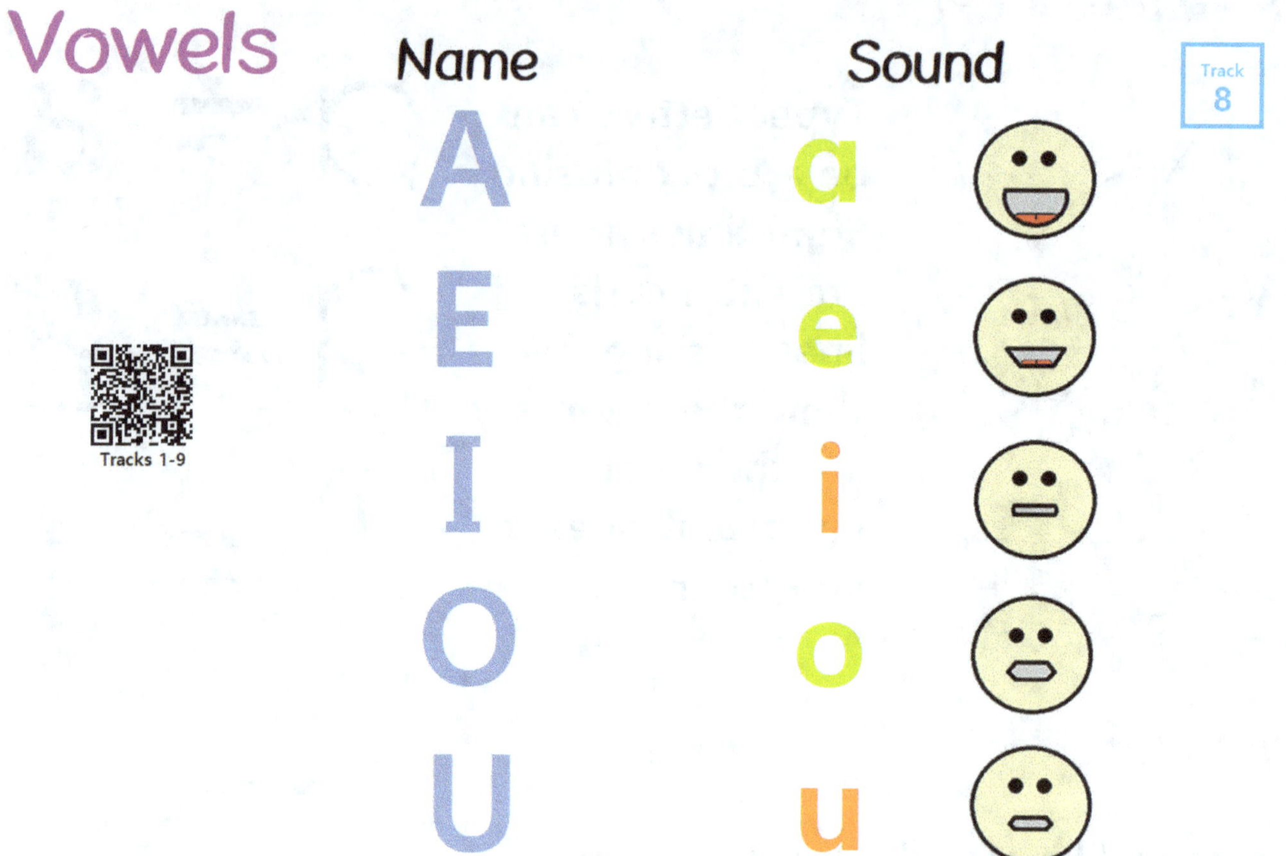

A · a
E · e
I · i
O · o
U · u

The name is long. The sound is short. i and u are VERY short.

Long and short sounds

Some letters can make a long sound, and some letters definitely can't! It's mportant to know which ones can make a long sound. We'll be learning that.

"Sometimes Sounds"

Tracks 10-19

Many letters have a "sometimes sound."
Sometimes the letter A makes the same
sound as the letter U!
You can hear it in the word "banana."
We use that sometimes sound for the word "a."

Practice with your teacher:

1. A banana

2. A cobra

3. A pizza

4. A panda

UNIT 1   Single-Letter Sounds

Listen, point, and make the sound

Tracks 10-19

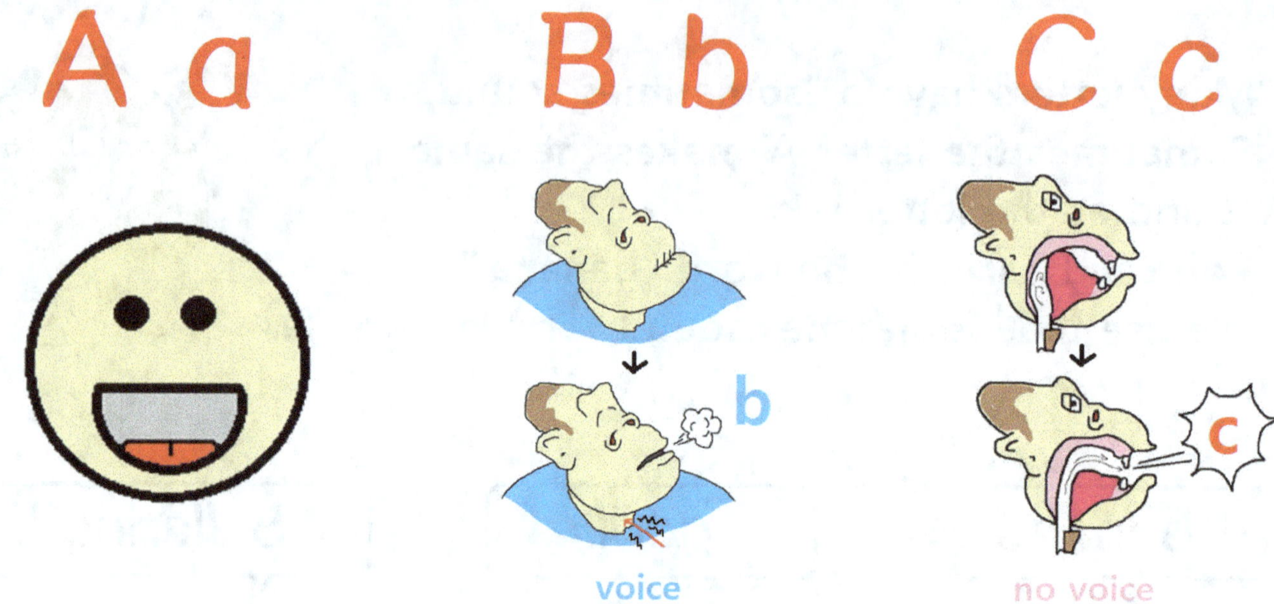

Listen and draw a line from the sound to the matching picture

Follow the rules

A

1 2 3

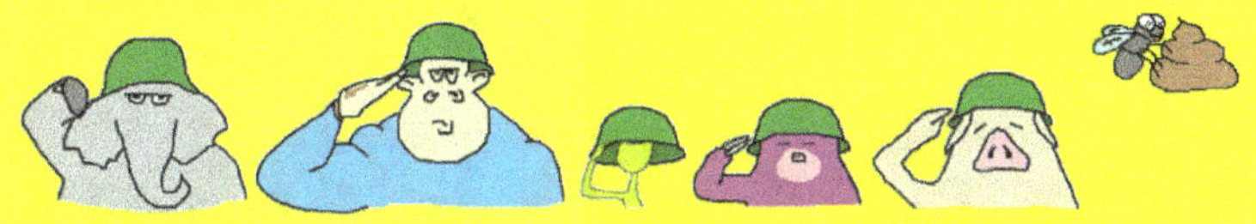

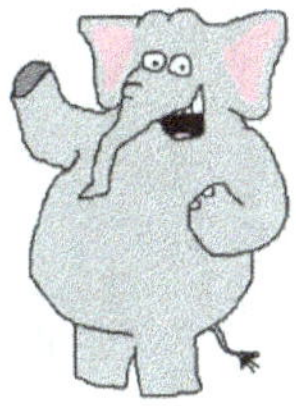

a

1 2

B

1 2

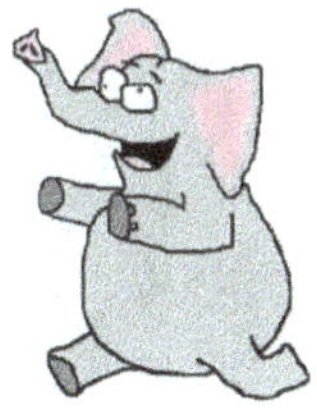

b

1 2

C

1

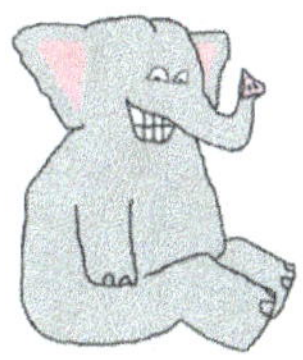

c

1

Listen, point and repeat the new words

Aa

Bb

Cc

Do it again..and again.. and again!

Writing practice

Word search   Listen and circle the word you hear

Track 14

Tracks 10-19

candy   apple   angry   bird   cat   baby

alligator   car   book   cup   banana   ant

Exercises

Circle the word you hear

Tracks 10-19

Track 15

Write the matching letter

Chant

Track 16

Sight words: a / an   and

An apple and a banana
An apple and a banana
An apple and a banana
And an angry cat

A cup and candy
A cup and candy
A cup and candy
And an angry bird

Circle the sound you hear

1. a b c
2. a b c
3. a b c
4. a b c
5. a b c
6. a b c

Listen and read along

Listen, point, and make the sound

Track 19

Tracks 10-19

D d   E e   F f

Listen and draw a line from the sound to the matching picture

Track 20

d   e   f

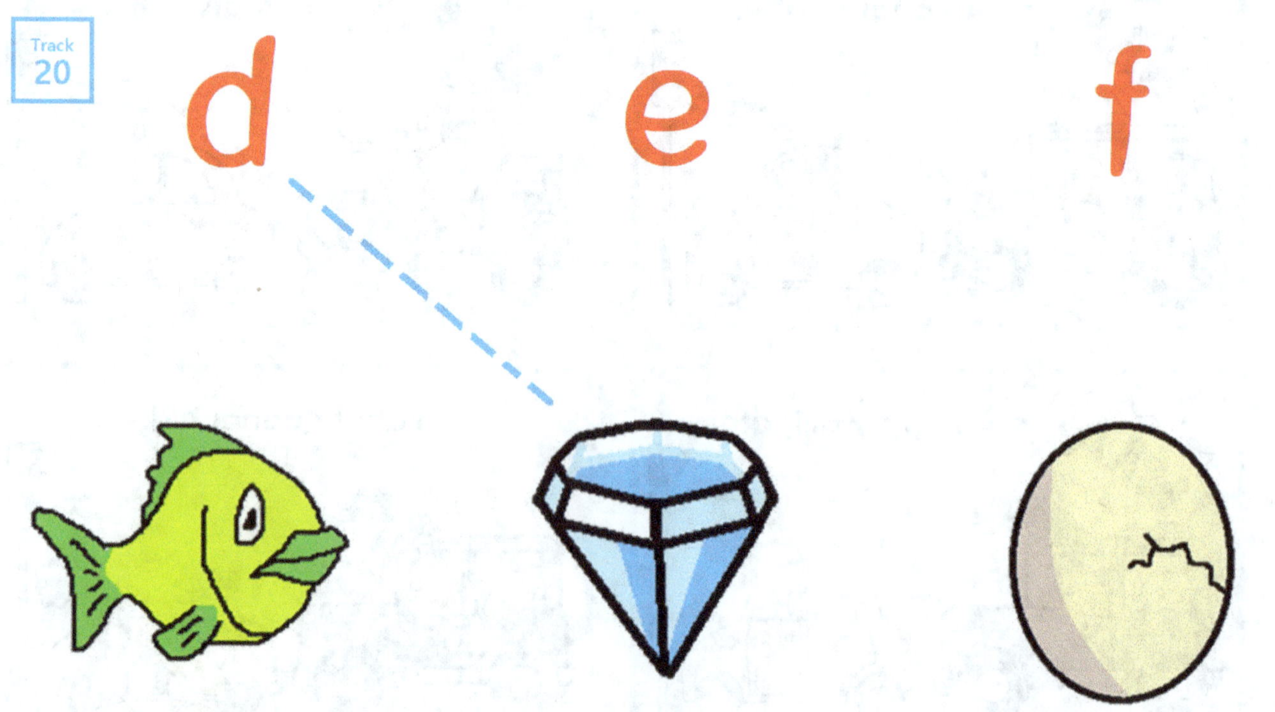

D  d

E e

F f

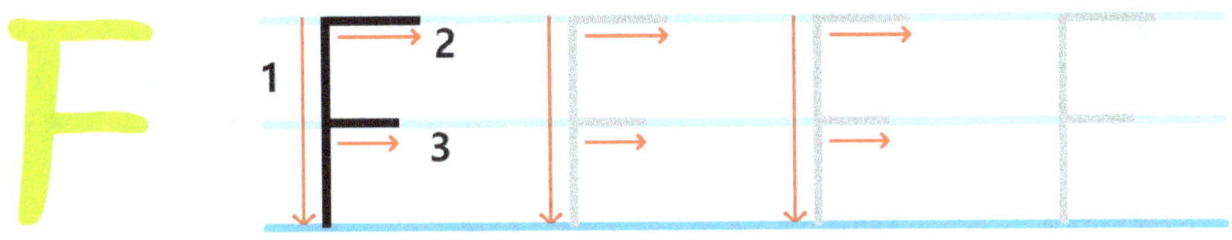

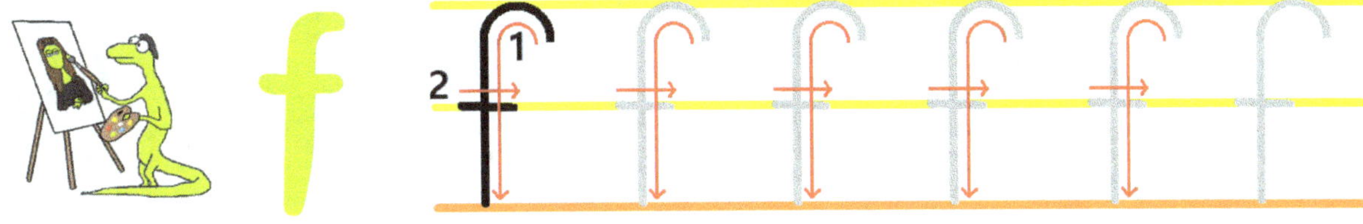

Listen, point and repeat the new words

Dd

Ee

Ff

Do it again..and again.. and again!

Exercises

Writing practice

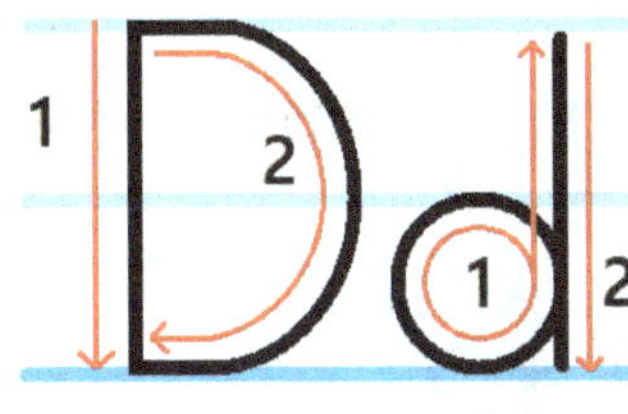
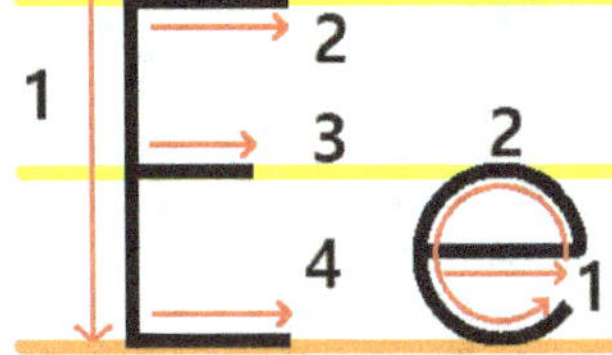
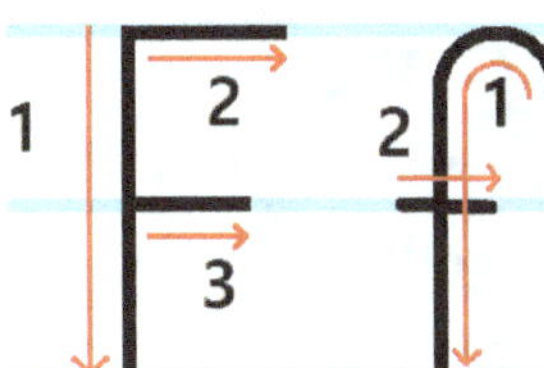

Word search   *Listen and circle the word you hear*   Track 22

Tracks 20-29

desk   **diamond**   **four**   **fish**   **flower**   **elephant**

elbow   **elf**   **dog**   **frog**   **door**   **egg**

Exercises

Circle the word you hear

Tracks 20-29

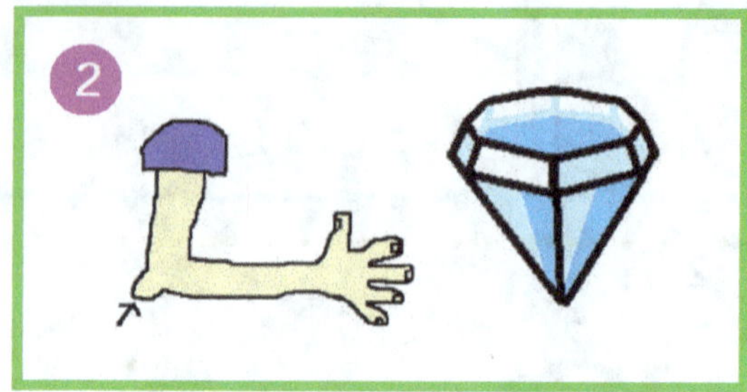

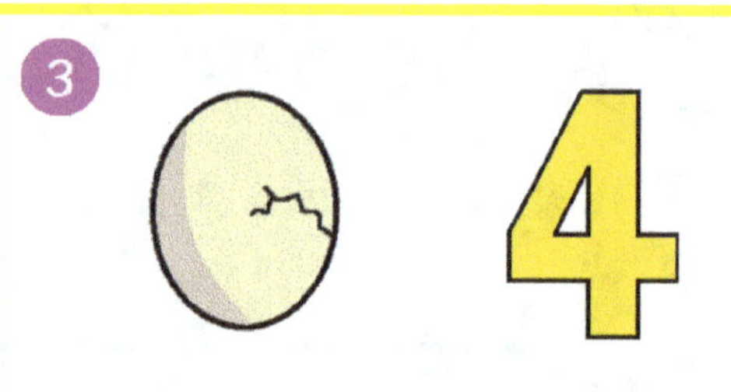

Write the matching letter

Chant

New sight words: all   on

A fish and a frog
And an elephant elbow
All on a diamond desk

A book and a cup
And an angry ant
All on a diamond desk

Story

Circle the sound you hear

Tracks 20-29

1. d e f
2. d e f
3. d e f
4. d e f
5. d e f
6. d e f

Listen and read along

New sight words: in   the

An elf in the flowers.

A dog in the flowers.

A dog-egg in the flowers.

An elf in the dog-egg!

Listen, point, and make the sound

Track 27

Listen and draw a line from the sound to the matching picture

Track 28

Follow the rules

G   g

H h

I i

New Words

Listen, point and repeat the new words

Tracks 20-29

Track 29

Gg

gold   good   gorilla   grass

Hh

happy   hat   hill   house

Ii

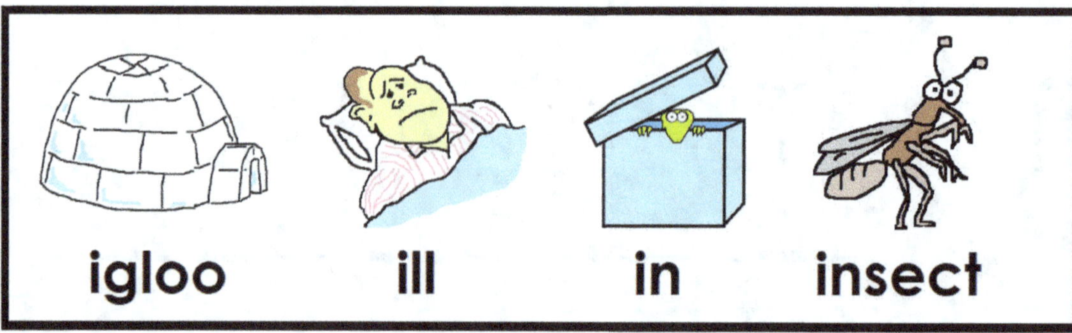

igloo   ill   in   insect

Do it again..and again.. and again!

Writing practice

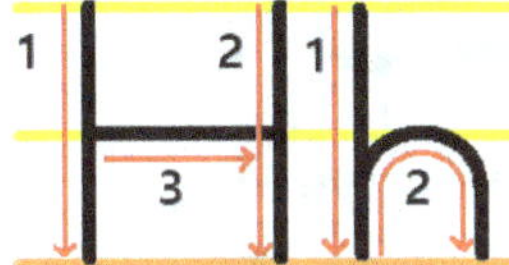

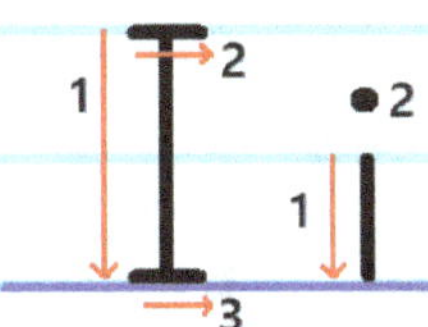

Word search   Listen and circle the word you hear

Track 30

Tracks 30-39

in   good   happy   grass   ill   house

gorilla   hat   igloo   hill   gold   insect

Exercises

Circle the word you hear

Track 31

Tracks 30-39

Write the matching letter

Chant

Track 32

Ill in a hat
Ill in a good hat
Ill in a good gold hat

Ill in a house
Ill in a good house
Ill in a good gold house

Story

Circle the sound you hear

Tracks 30-39

1	g h i	2	g h i
3	g h i	4	g h i
5	g h i	6	g h i

Listen and read along

New sight words: no

Grass on a hill.

A happy insect in the grass.

A happy gorilla on a hill.

No happy insect in the grass.

Listen, point, and make the sound

J j   K k   L l

Listen and draw a line from the sound to the matching picture

j   k   l

Follow the rules

J J J J J

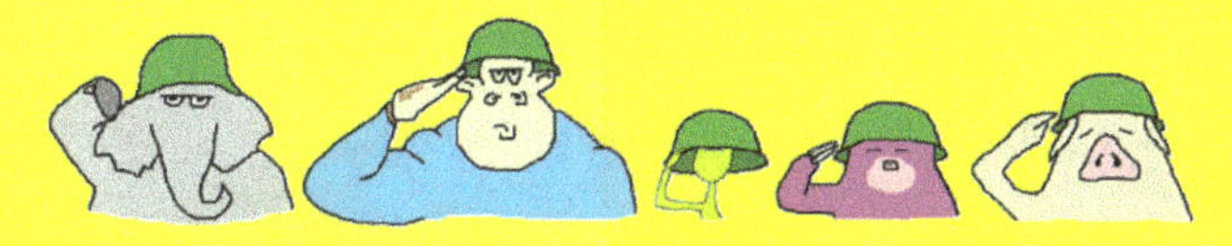

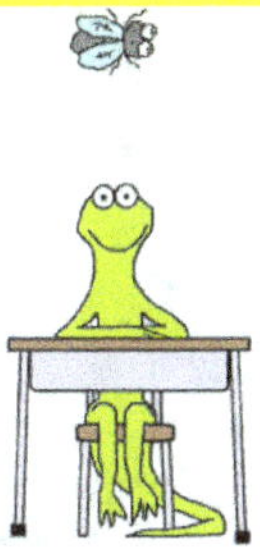

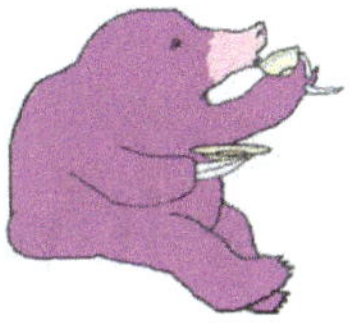

j j j j j j j

K K K K K

k k k k k k k

L L L L L

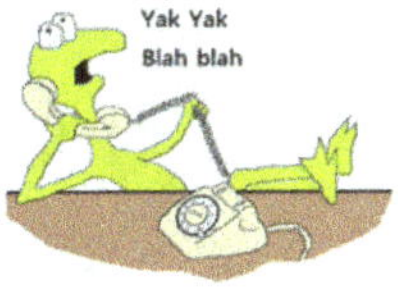

l l l l l l l

New Words

Listen, point and repeat the new words

Track
37

J j

jail   jam   jet   jump

K k

kangaroo   key   kick   kite

L l

leg   lemon   lid   lion

Do it again..and again.. and again!

Writing practice

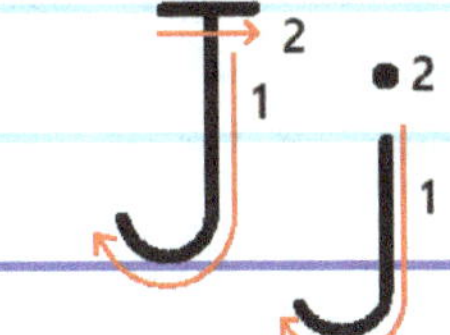

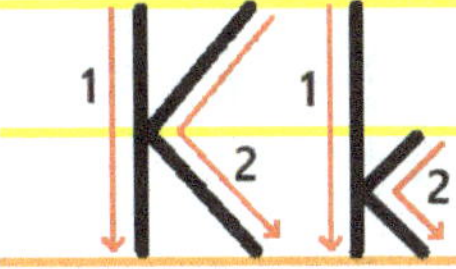

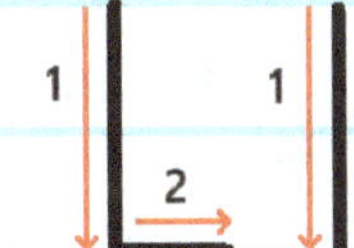

Word search   Listen and circle the word you hear

Tracks 30-39

lion   **jam**   **jet**   **lid**   **kangaroo**   **jump**

leg   **kite**   **jail**   **lemon**   **key**   **kick**

Exercises

Circle the word you hear

Write the matching letter

Chant

New sight words: lift like

Lemon jam
Lemon jam
Lift the lid
Kangaroos like lemon jam

Kangaroo jam
Kangaroo jam
Lift the lid
Lions like kangaroo jam

34   Unit 4

Story

Circle the sound you hear

Tracks 40-49

1. j k l   2. j k l

3. j k l   4. j k l

5. j k l   6. j k l

Listen and read along

New sight words: get

Lion and kangaroo in jail.

Kick the leg! Get the key!

Jump in the jet!

Lion in jail.

Review

Listen, point, and say

A a 

B b 

C c 

D d 

E e 

F f 

G g 

H h 

I i 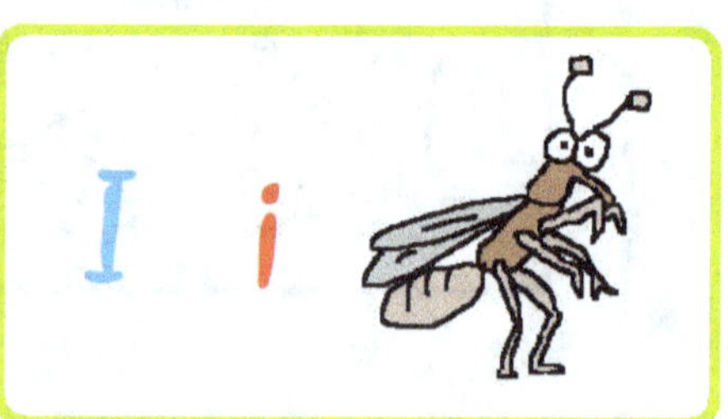

J j 

K k 

L l 

Review

Say all the words and write the letter

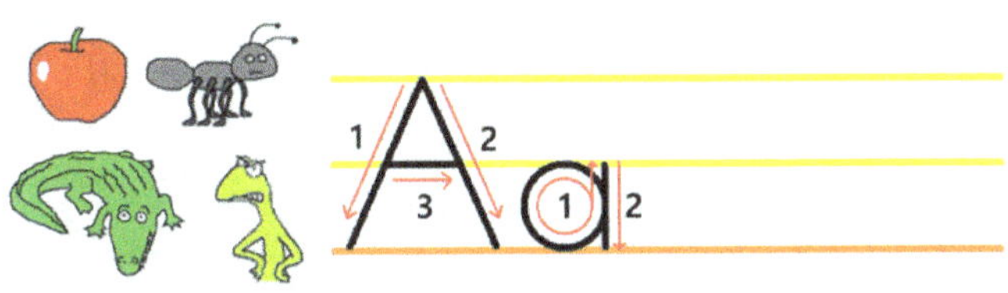 A a

 B b

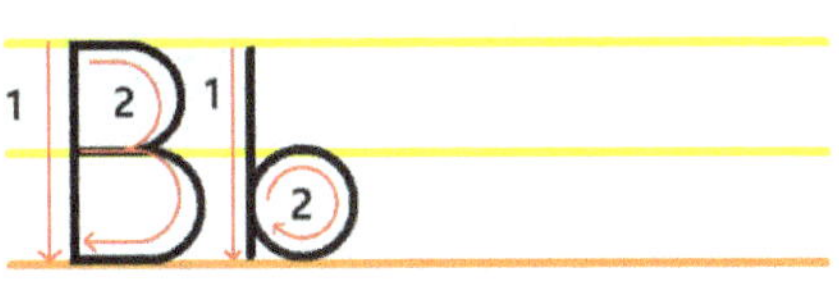

 C c

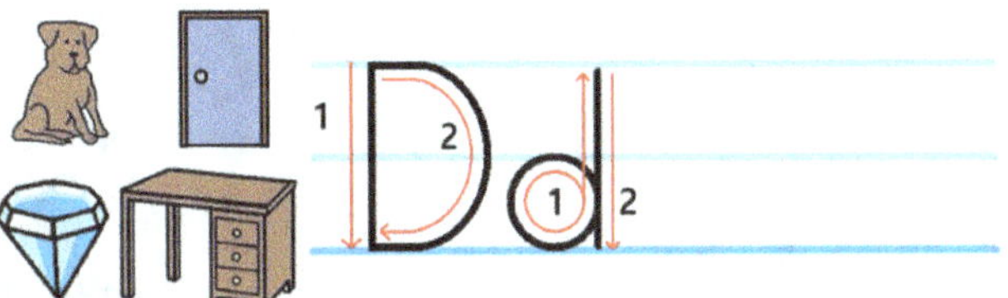 D d

 E e

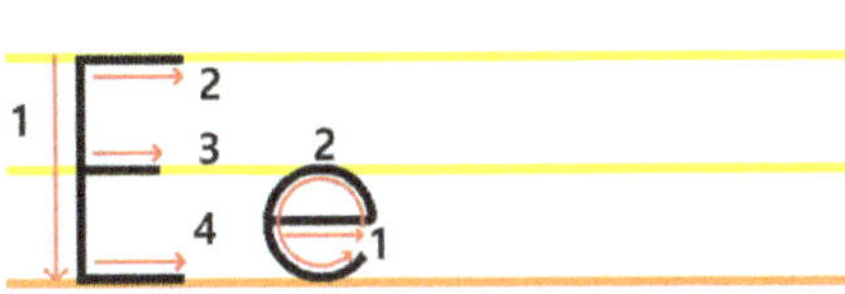

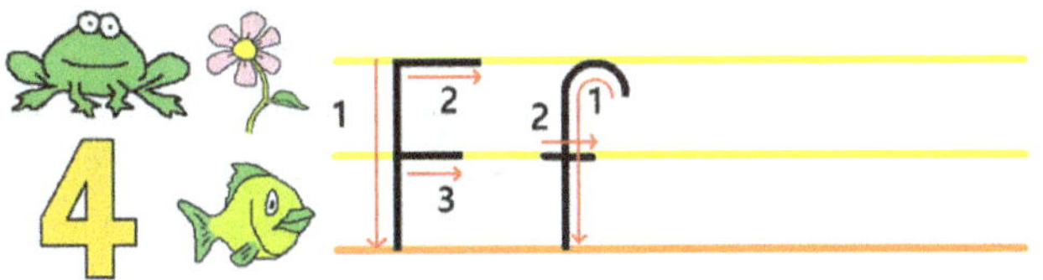 F f

 G g

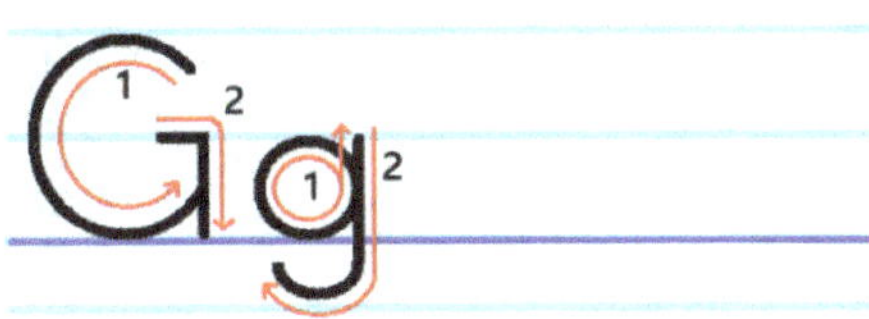

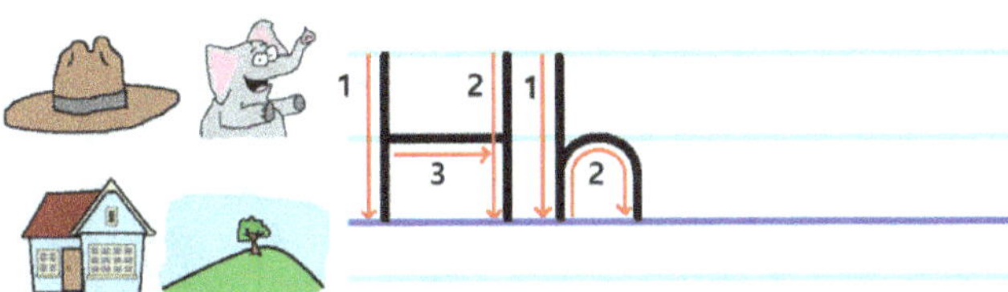 H h

 I i

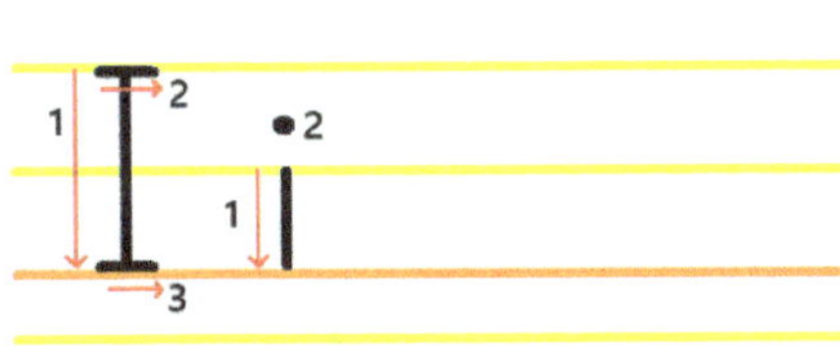

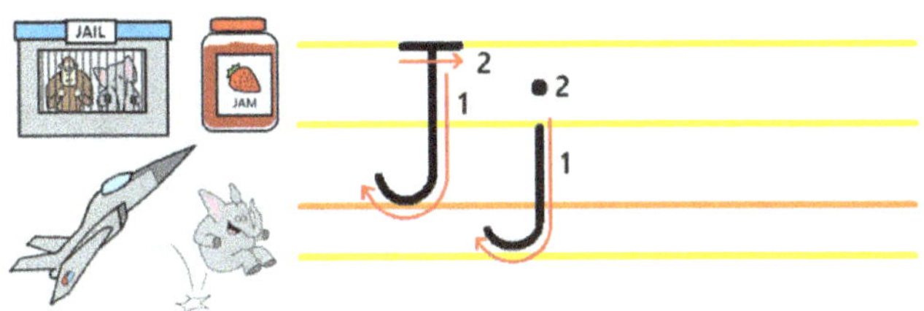 J j

 K k

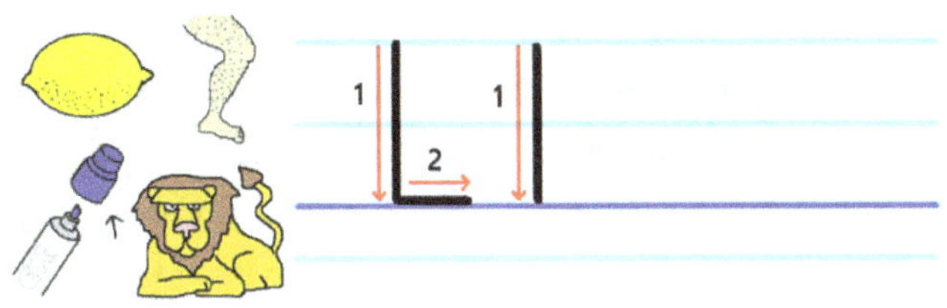 L l

Review

Find the path

1 H   a

2 A   h

3 G   d

4 D   g

Listen and circle the matching letter

Tracks 40-49

1  d e f   2  i h j

3 i g k   4 j k l

5 a c f   6 d h b

Listen and circle. Then write the word

Tracks 40-49

1  

elf

2  

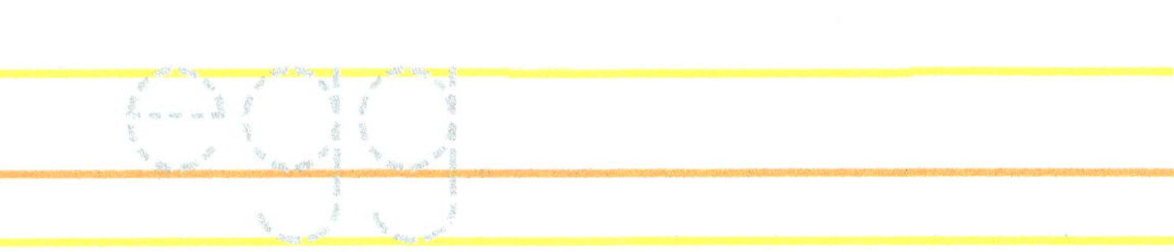

egg

3  

kick

4  

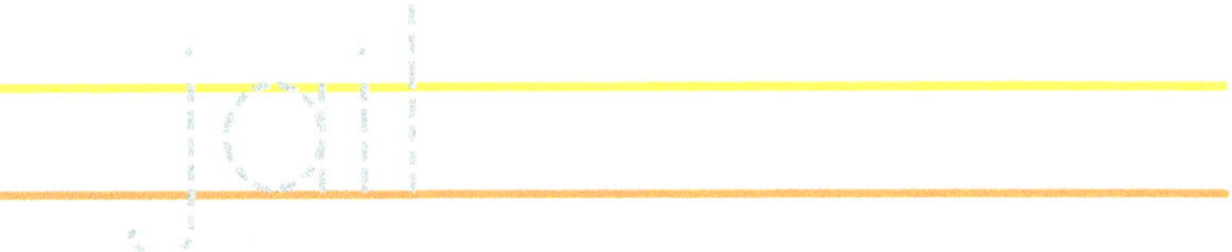

jail

5  

gold

More Sounds

"Sometimes Sounds"

Tracks 40-49

Track
46

Sometimes when a vowel begins a word,
we use its name, not its sound.

apple

acorn

egg

eagle

in

ice-cream

on

old

up

unicorn

Syllables

Tracks 40-49

Have you noticed that
words have a rythm?

"Banana" has 3 beats, but
we don't say "beats" for
words. We say "syllables."

(Not silly bulls)

Not everyone uses the same syllables.

1   2   3
cam/er/a

1   2
cam/era

1   2   3
di/a/mond

1   2
di/amond

UNIT 5   Single-Letter Sounds

Listen, point, and make the sound

Tracks 40-49

Track 49

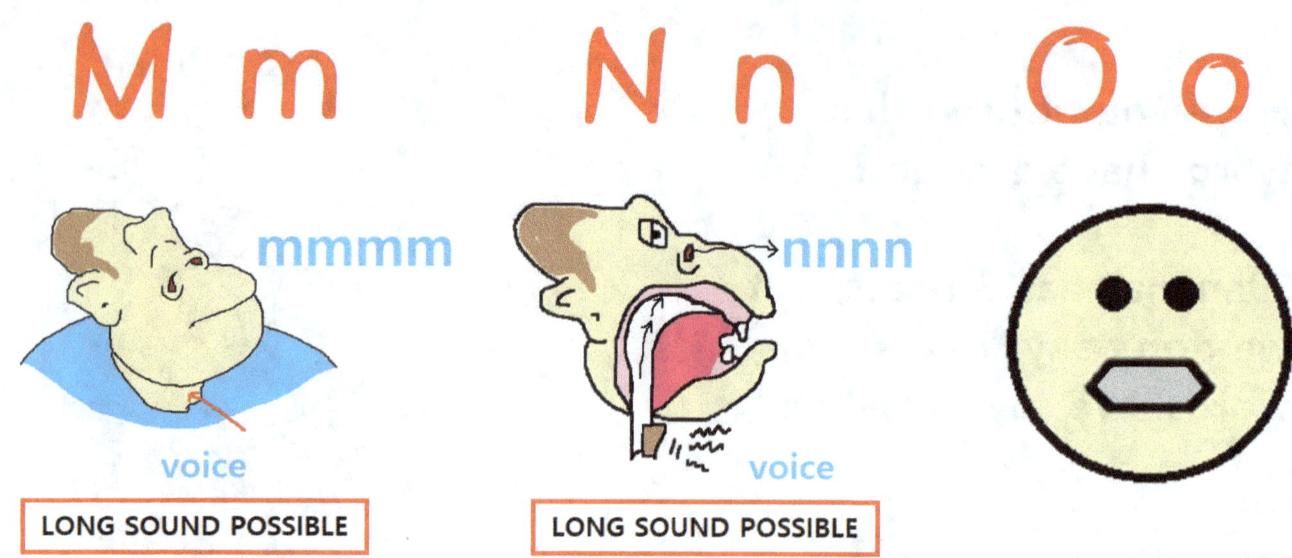

Listen and draw a line from the sound to the matching picture

Track 50

Follow the rules

M   m

N n

O o

New Words

Listen, point and repeat the new words

Track
51

milk   **monkey**   **moon**   **mouse**

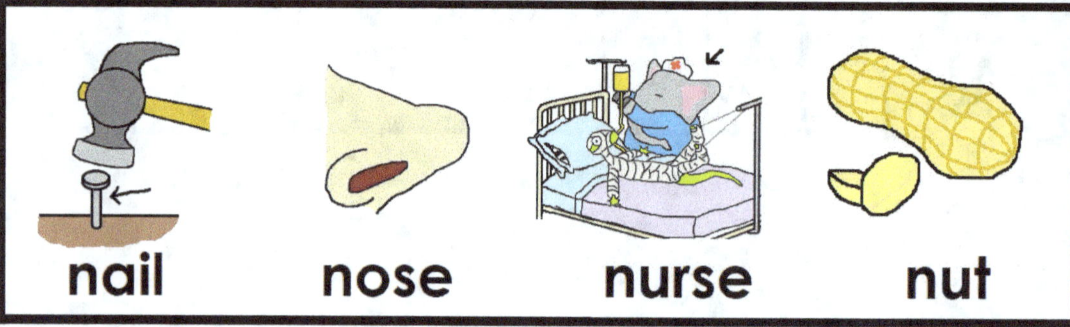

nail   **nose**   **nurse**   **nut**

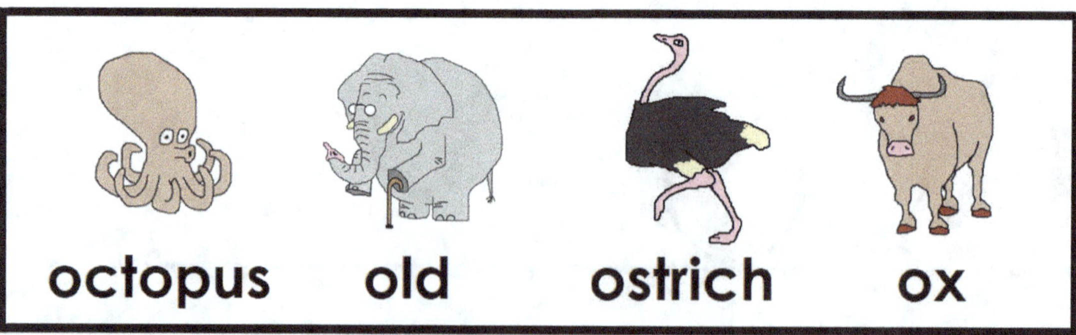

octopus   **old**   **ostrich**   **ox**

Do it again..and again.. and again!

Exercises

Writing practice

Word search 

Listen and circle the word you hear

Track 52

Tracks 50-59

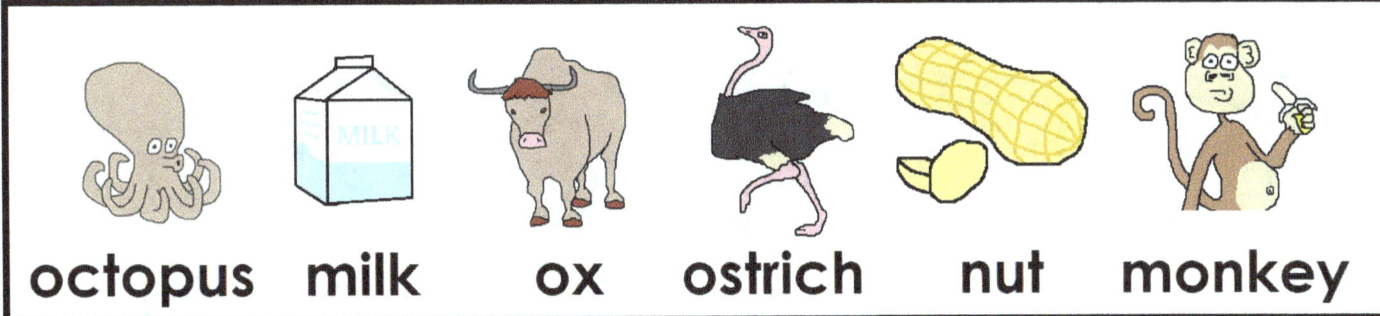

octopus   **milk**   **ox**   **ostrich**   **nut**   **monkey**

nail   **old**   **nurse**   **moon**   **nose**   **mouse**

Exercises

Circle the word you hear

Tracks 50-59

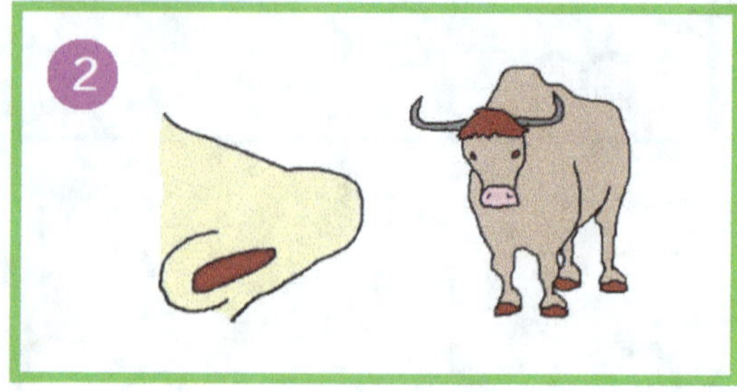

Write the matching letter

Chant

New sight words:　oh not

Old monkey milk
And an octopus nose

Old monkey milk
And an octopus nose

Oh no! Oh no!
Not old monkey millk!

Story

Circle the sound you hear

1. m   n   o   2. m   n   o

3. m   n   o   4. m   n   o

5. m   n   o   6. m   n   o

Listen and read along

Ox and mouse and ostrich on the moon.

A nail!   Get the nail!

Oh no. Not good.

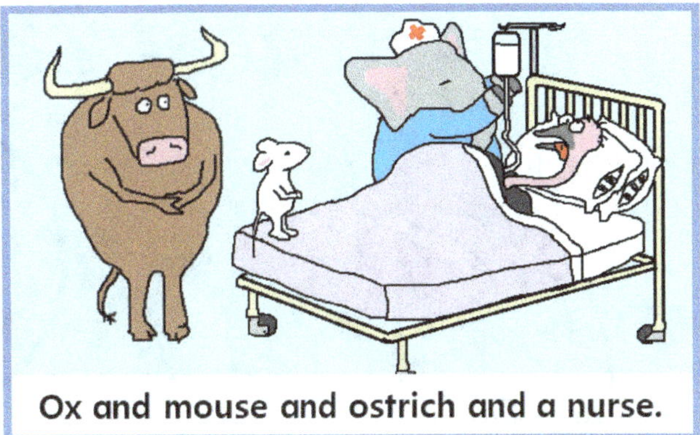
Ox and mouse and ostrich and a nurse.

Listen, point, and make the sound

Tracks 50-59

Track 57

Listen and draw a line from the sound to the matching picture

Track 58

p   q   r

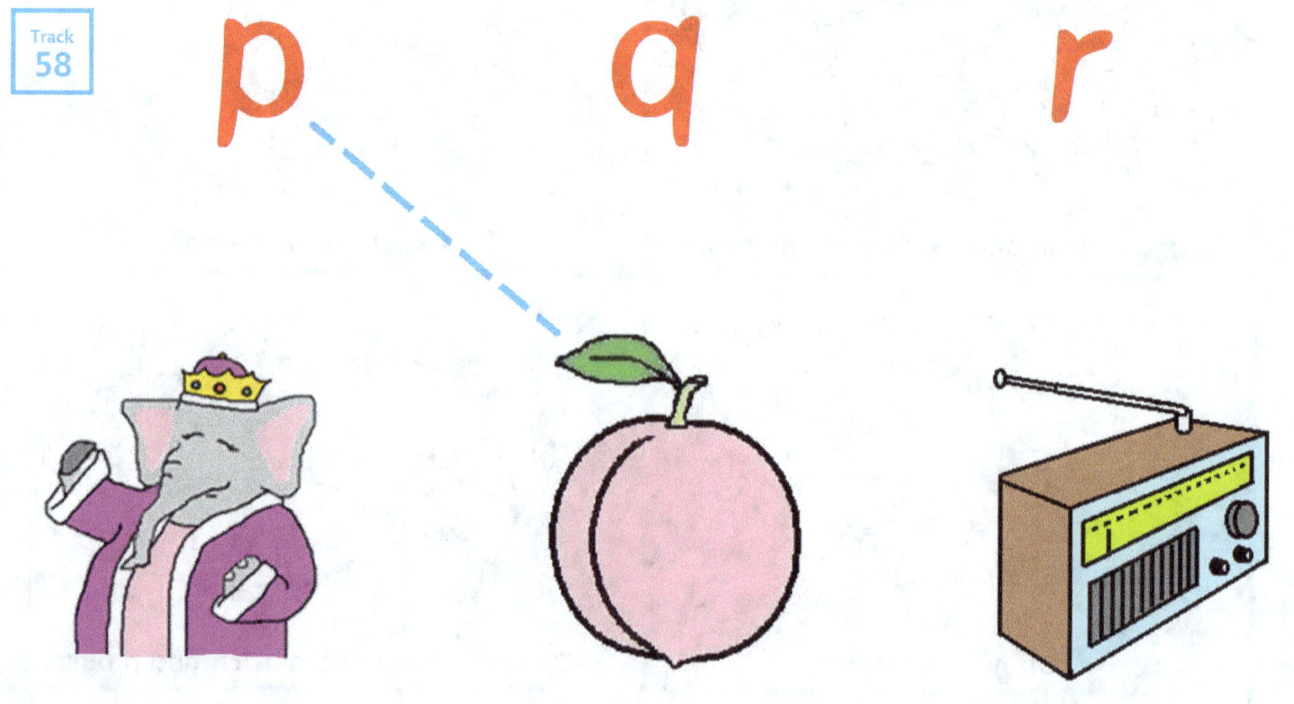

Follow the rules

P P P P P

p p p p p p

Q Q Q Q Q

q q q q q q

R R R R R

r r r r r r

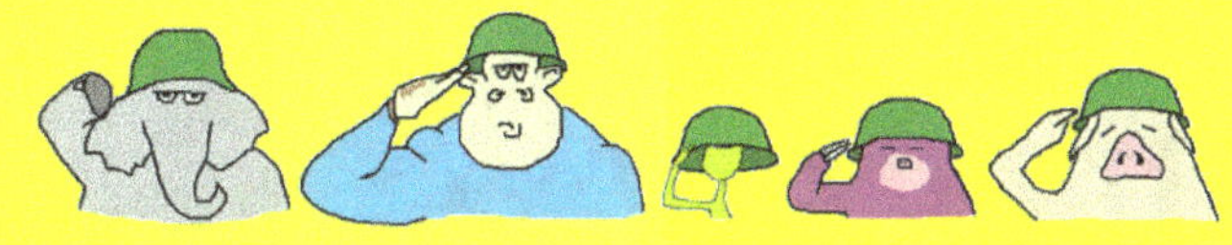

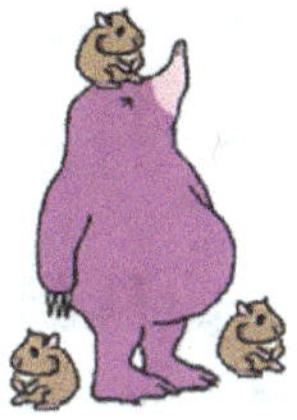

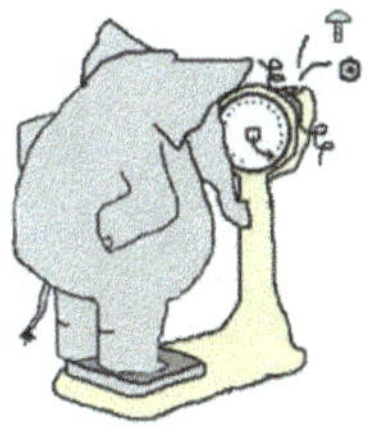

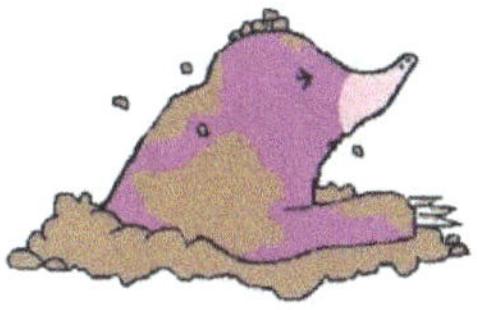

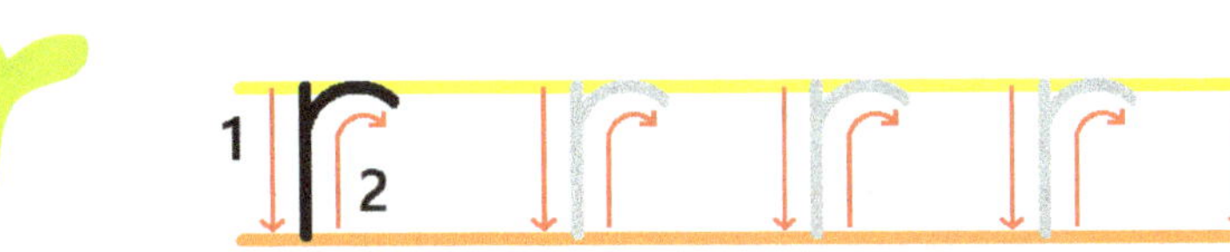

New Words

Tracks 50-59

Pp

Qq

Rr

Do it again..and again.. and again!

Exercises

Writing practice

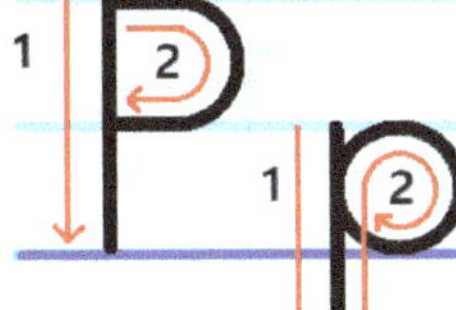

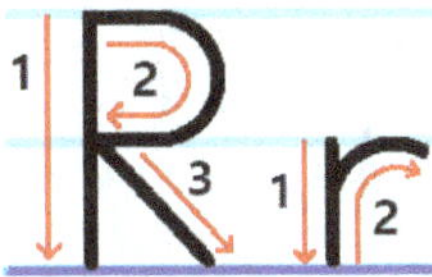

Word search   Listen and circle the word you hear

Tracks 60-69

Exercises

Circle the word you hear

Track 61

Tracks 60-69

1

2

3

4

Write the matching letter

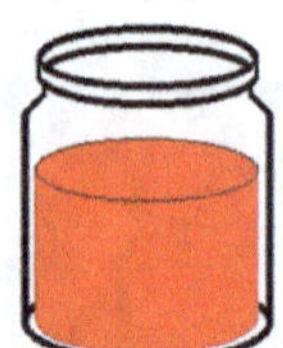

Chant

Track 62

New sight words: did   you   your

A quick quiet question:

Did you poop your pants?

A quick quiet question:

Did you poop your pants?

Circle the sound you hear

Track 63

Tracks 60-69

1. p q r   2. p q r

3. p q r   4. p q r

5. p q r   6. p q r

Listen and read along

Track 64

New sight words: has   put

Listen, point, and make the sound

Tracks 60-69

Track 65

S s   T t   U u   V v

Listen and draw a line from the sound to the matching picture

s   t   u   v

Track 66

Follow the rules

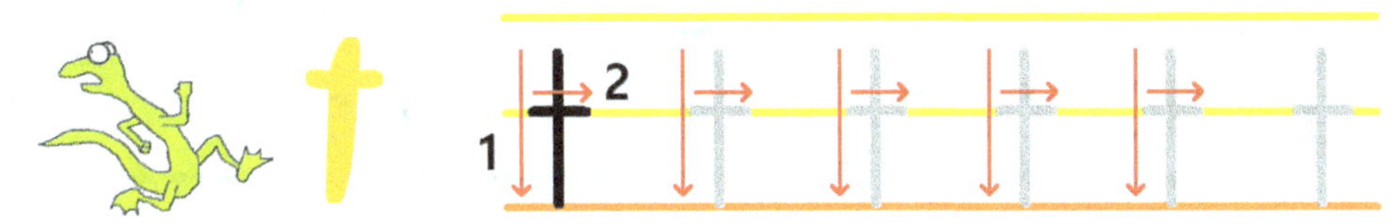

New Words

Tracks 60-69

Track 67

Ss

sad   sit   smell   sun

Tt

tear   ten   tiger   time

Uu

umbrella   umpire   under   up

Vv

van   vest   violin   vomit

Do it again..and again.. and again!

Exercises

Writing practice

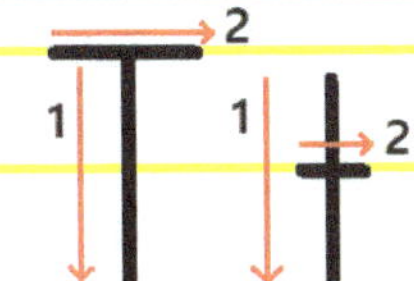

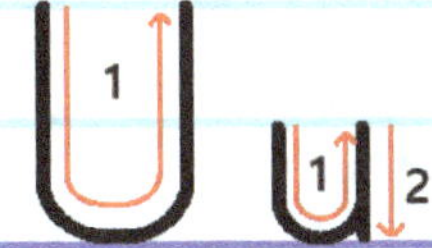

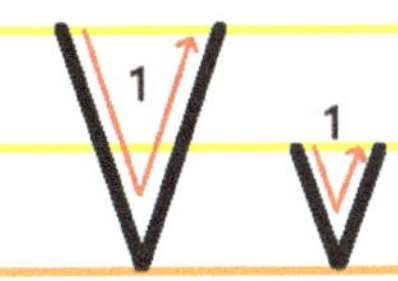

Word search   Listen and circle the word you hear

Tracks 60-69

      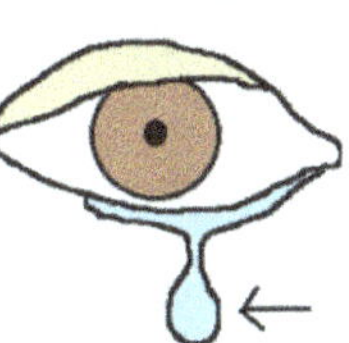

sad   under   up   ten   vest   van   smell   tear

sit   time   sun   umbrella   tiger   vomit   violin   umpire

Exercises

Circle the word you hear

Track **69**

Tracks 60-69

1

2

3

4

Write the matching letter

   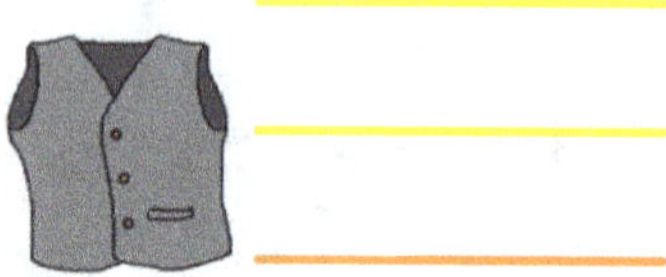

Chant

Track **70**

New words: one   by   fella (fellow)

Sad tiger sits
Under the sun,
Tiger tears, tiger tears,
One by one.

Sad tiger sits
Under an umbrella,
Violins! Violins!
Sad, sad fella.

Story

Circle the sound you hear

Tracks 70-79

1. s t u v
2. s t u v
3. s t u v
4. s t u v
5. s t u v
6. s t u v

Listen and read along

New sight words: says go to win

UNIT 8   Single-Letter Sounds

Listen, point, and make the sound

Track 73

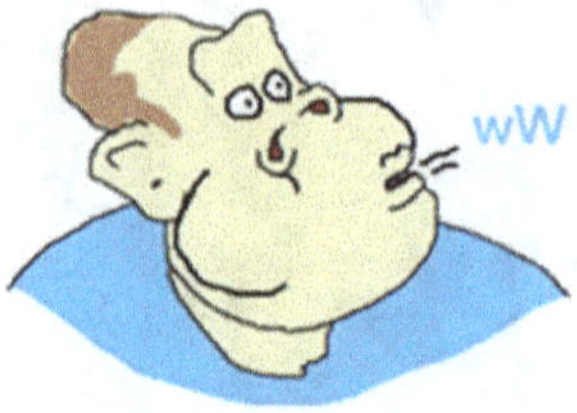

Tracks 70-79

W w   X x   Y y   Z z

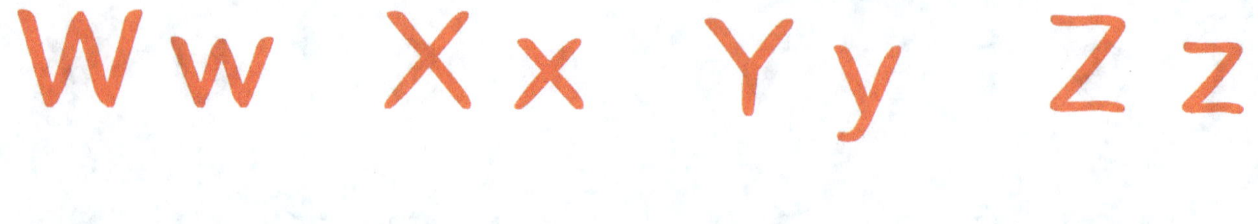

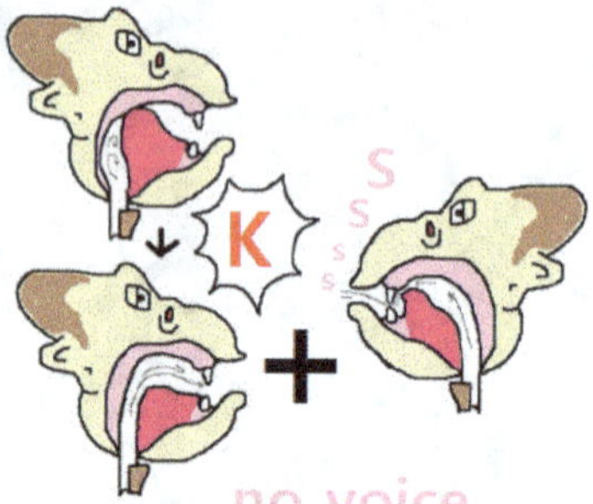

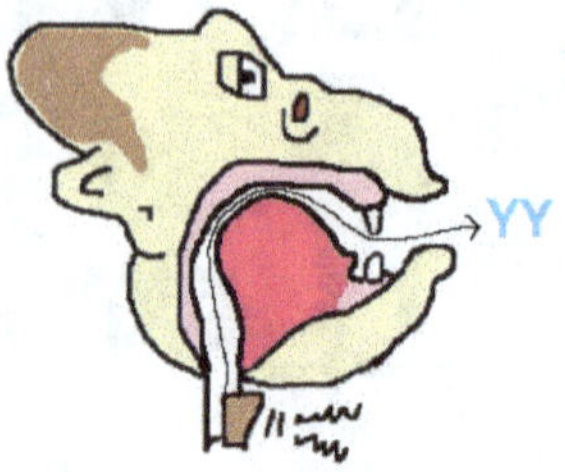

Listen and draw a line from the sound to the matching picture

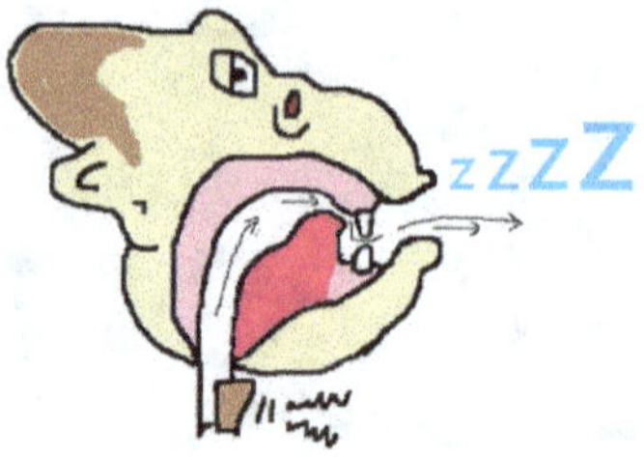

W   X   y   Z

Track 74

Follow the rules

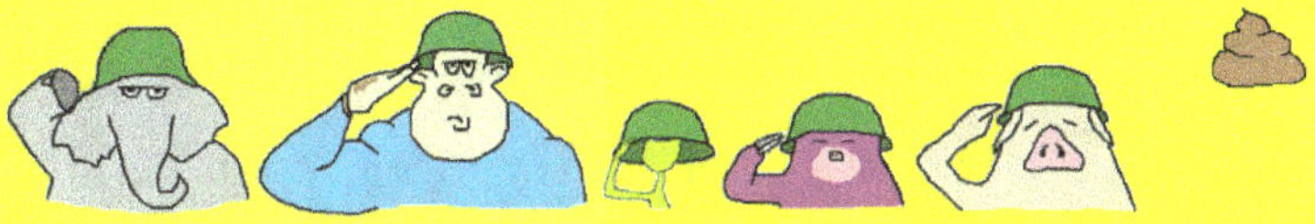

W W 1

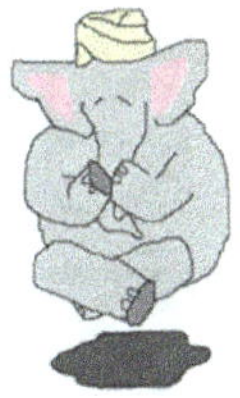

w w 1

X X 1 2

x x 1 2

Y Y 1 2 3

y y 1 2

Z Z 1

z z 1

New Words

Listen, point and repeat the new words

Ww

water   **wave**   **window**   **wish**

Xx

box   **fix**   **fox**   **six**

Yy

yawn   **yellow**   **young**   **yo-yo**

Zz

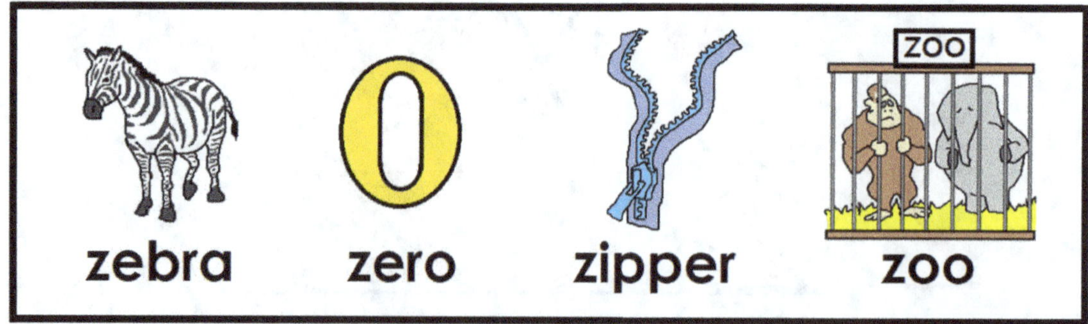

zebra   **zero**   **zipper**   **zoo**

Do it again..and again.. and again!

Writing practice

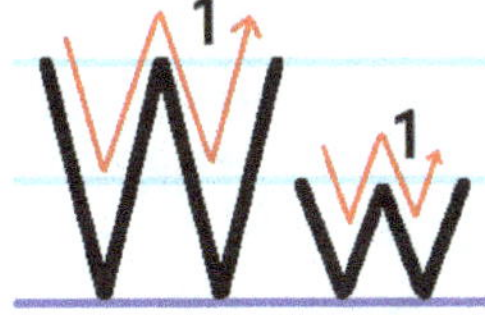

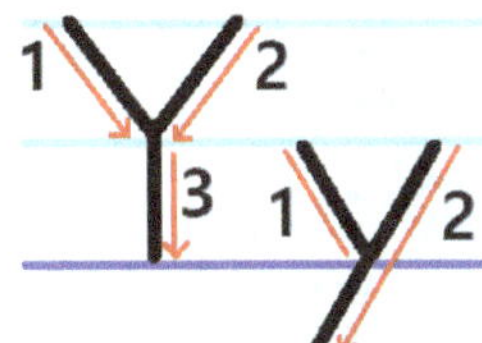

Word search Listen and circle the word you hear

Track 76

Tracks 70-79

window   zero   young   wave   yellow   zipper   yo-yo   box

fix   zebra   zoo   water   fox   yawn   six   wish

Exercises

Circle the word you hear

Tracks 70-79

Write the matching letter

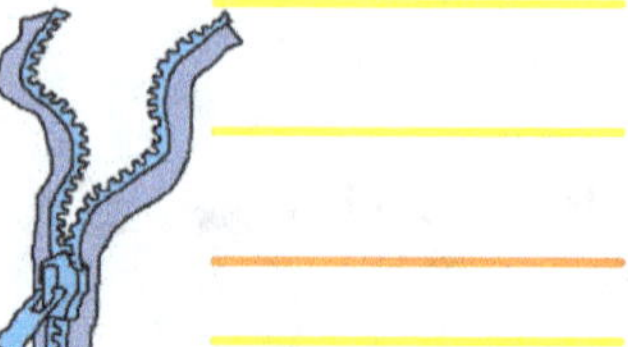

Chant

New sight words: I   had   it

I wish I had a zebra,

I wish I had a fox,

I wish I had a yo yo,

All in a yellow box,

I wish I did,

I wish I did,

I wish it had a yellow lid!

Story

Circle the sound you hear

1. w x y z   2. w x y z

3. w x y z   4. w x y z

5. w x y z   6. w x y z

Listen and read along

New sight words: wait

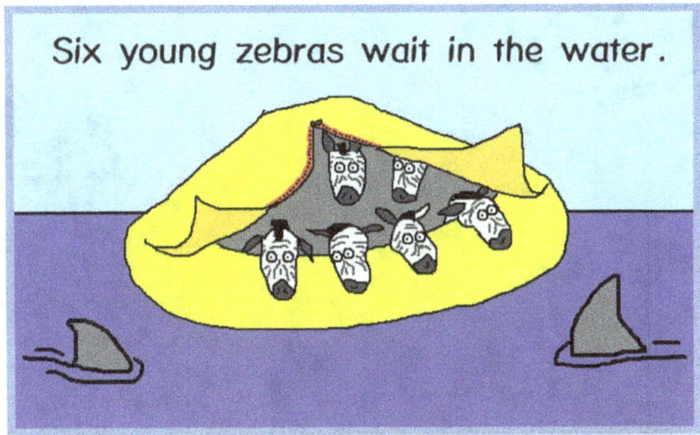

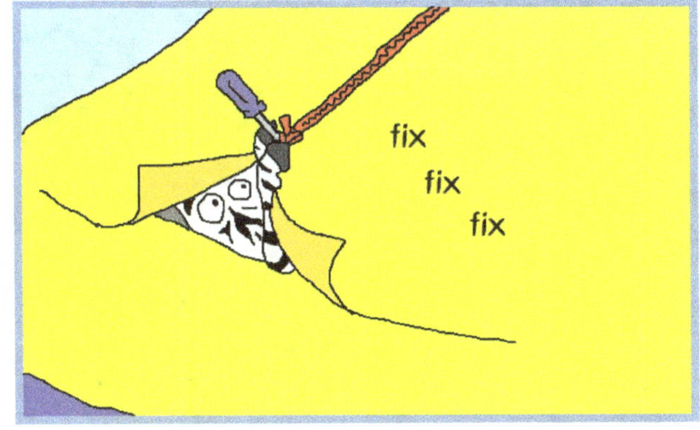

Unit 8   65

Review

Listen, point, and say

M m

N n

O o

P p

Q q

R r

S s

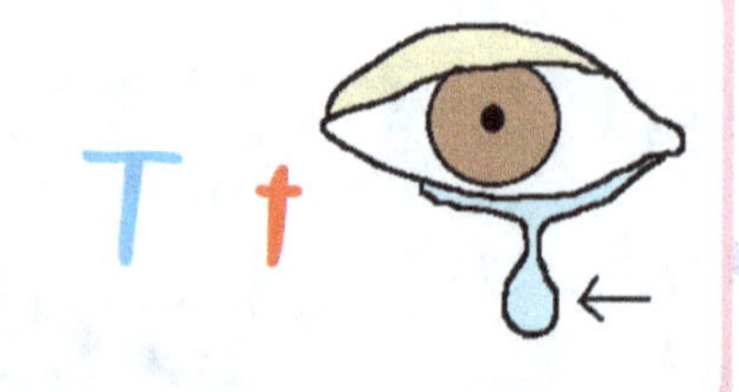

T t

U u

V v

W w

X x

Y y

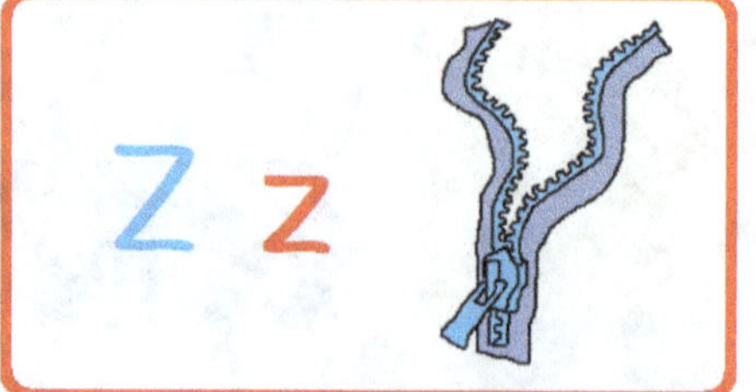

Z z

Review

 M m

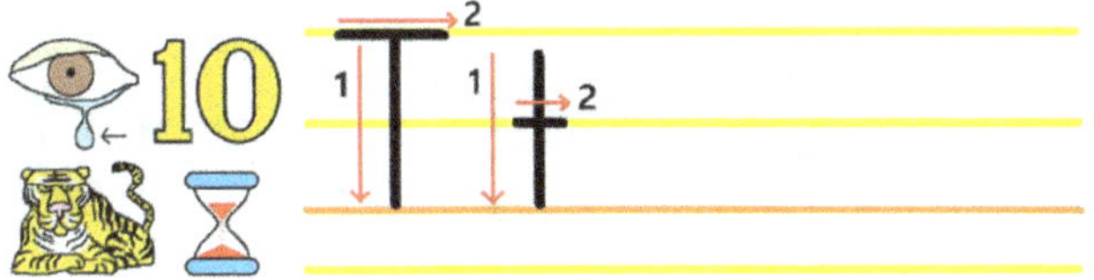 T t

 N n

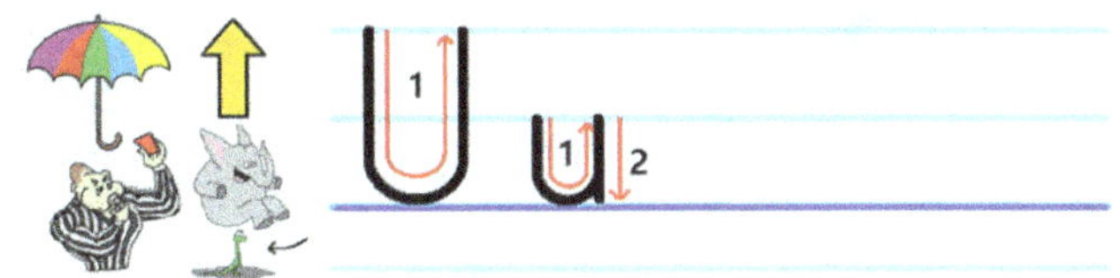 U u

 O o

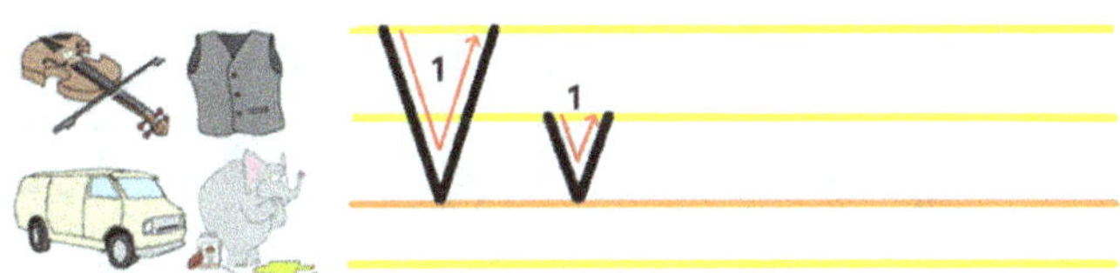 V v

 P p

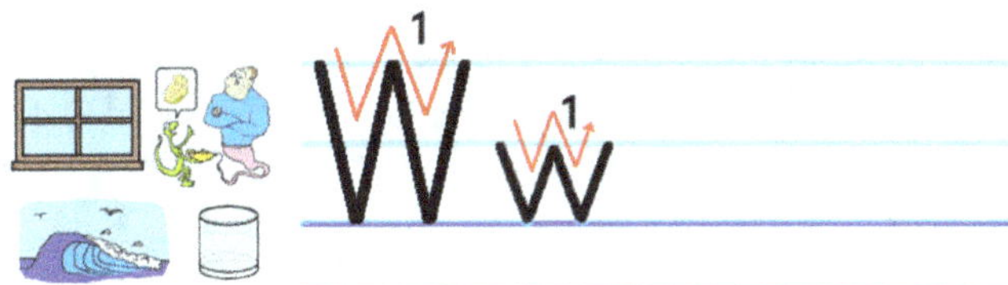 W w

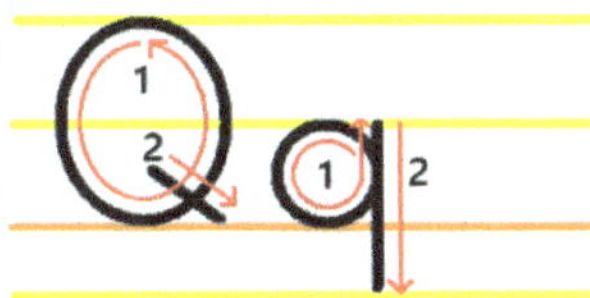 Q q

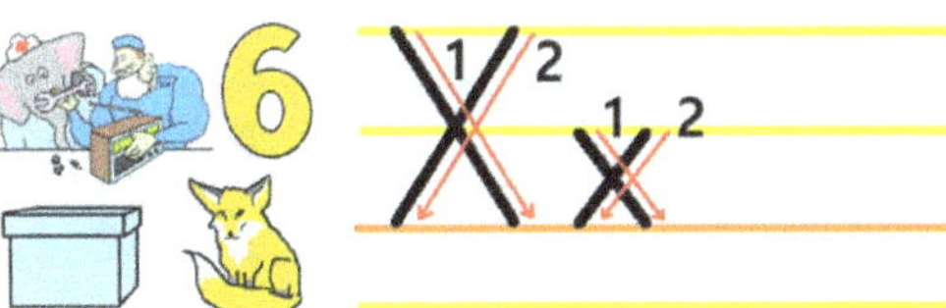 X x

 R r

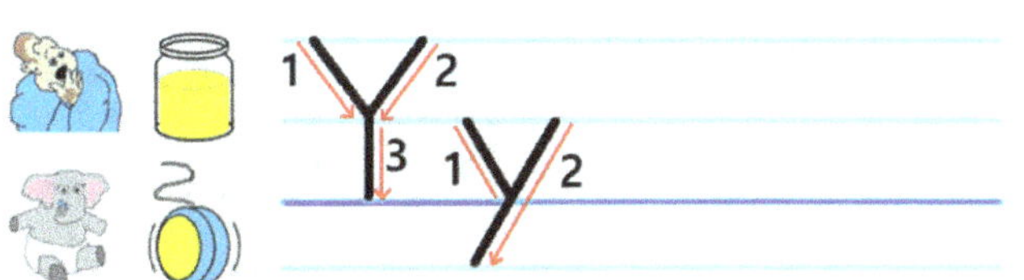 Y y

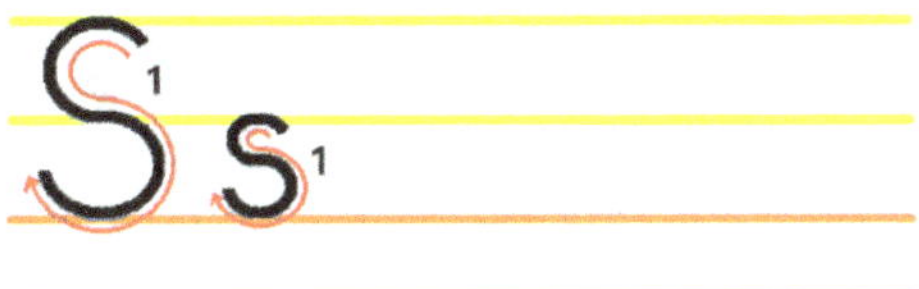 S s

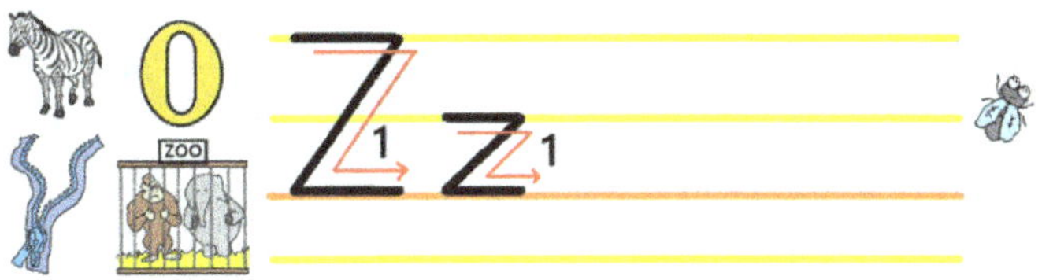 Z z

Review

Find the path

Listen and circle the matching letter

Track
82

Tracks 80-89

1		m s v	2		p s z
3		r n t	4		y u w
5		o q x	6		m t p

Review

Write the word twice

1 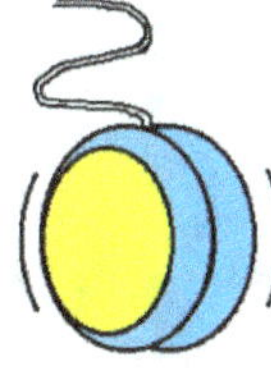 yoyo

2  nut

3  wave

4  time

5  mouse

6  vest

Listen, find, and circle

1 **bird** 2 **egg** 3 **run** 4 **candy** 5 **milk**
6 **zebra** 7 **fish** 8 **time** 9 **door** 10 **hat**

 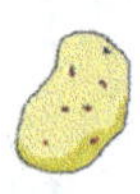    

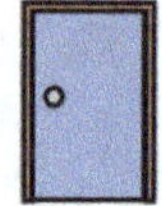     

Review 

Find the wrong ones and cross them out
(Say the first letter of each word... is it right?)

1 cup six potato four leg

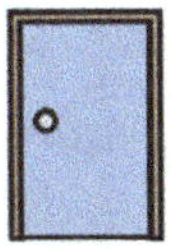

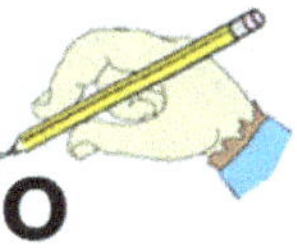

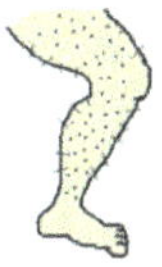

2 wave gorilla kick house kite

3 jump poop fox kangaroo lemon

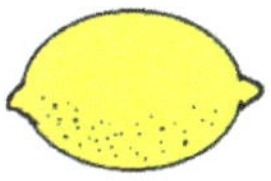

4 mouse queen banana lion in

5 car jam  fish time insect

Test

Tracks 80-89

Listen and circle the word you hear

a  Track 84 b  Track 85 c Track 86

1       

2      

3      

4     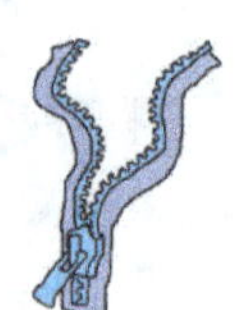 

5   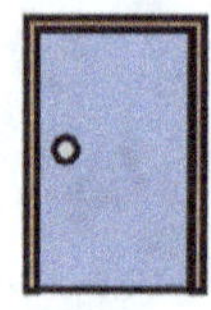   

6      

Listen and write the sound you hear a b c

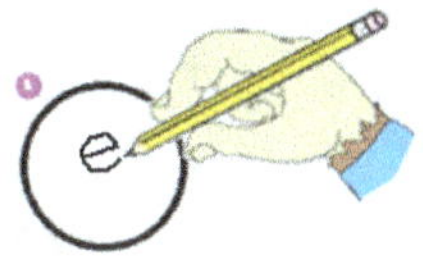

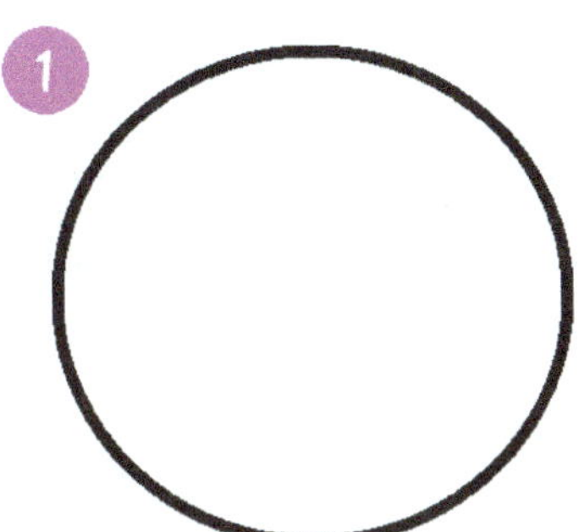

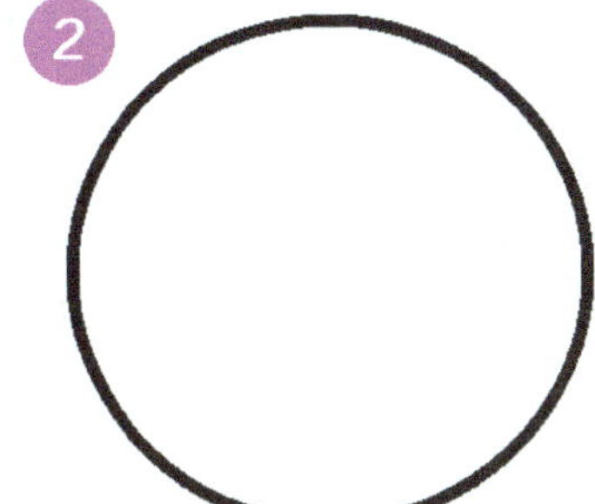

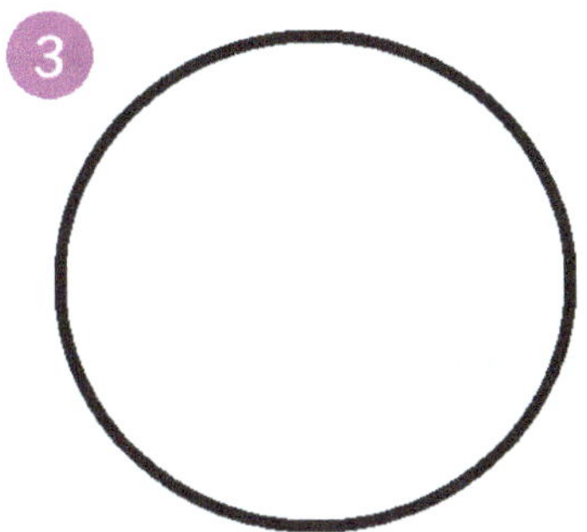

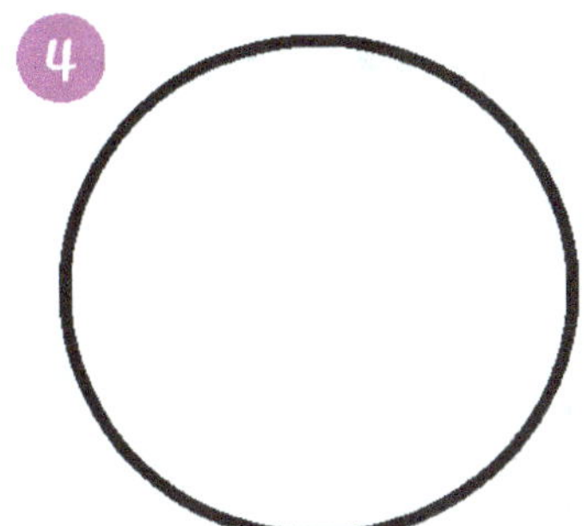

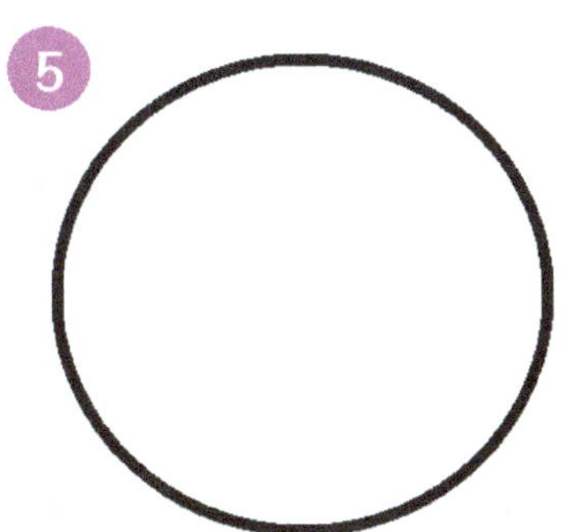

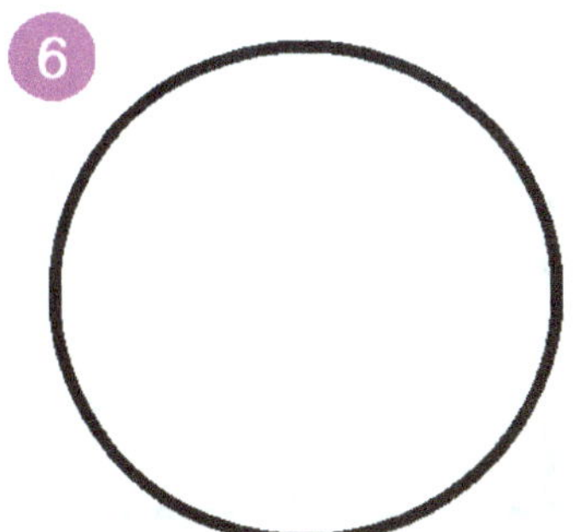

Test

Write the letter to match the picture

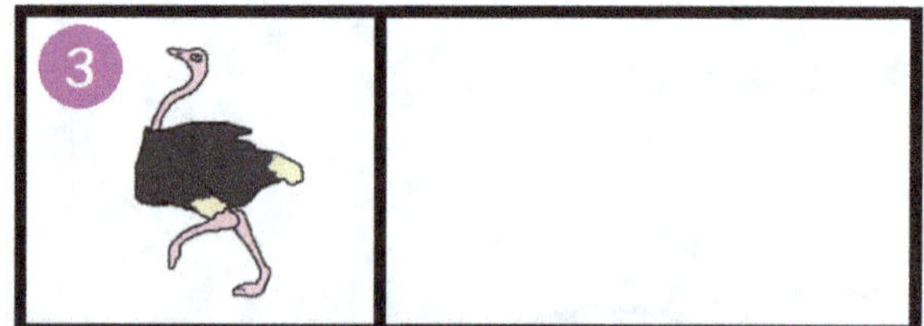

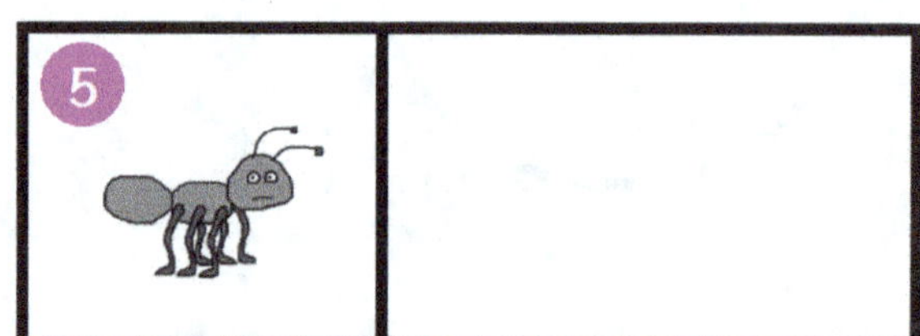

Listen and circle the sound you hear a Track 90 b Track 91 c Track 92

Tracks 90-93

1  j c f w o

2  a g n d i

3  o h x s l

4  u b e z q

5  p k m r a

6  h y v t g

CONGRATULATIONS!!

Now you know your alphabet sounds..

You can sing the

Alphabet Sound Song!!

Listen and sing along..if you can! Track 93

Tracks 90-93

a b c d e f g

h i j k  

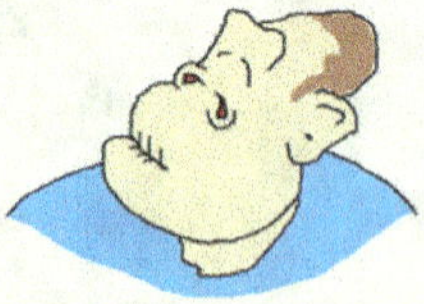

l m n o p

q r s t u v

w x y and z

How did you do?

This is the end of the book!

Word List

Unit 1

alligator

angry

ant

apple

baby

banana

bird

book

candy

car

cat

cup

Unit 2

desk

diamond

dog

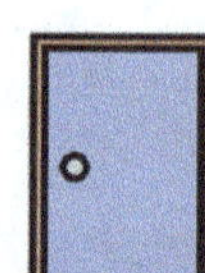
door

egg

elbow

elephant

elf

fish

flower

four

frog

Word List

Unit 3

gold

good

gorilla

grass

happy

hat

hill

house

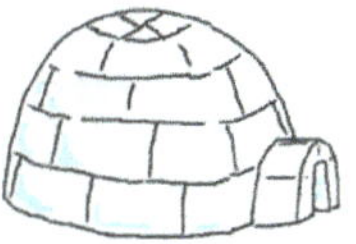
igloo

ill

in

insect

Unit 4

jail

jam

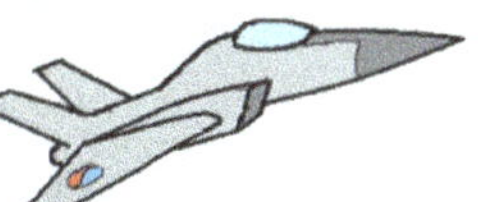
jet

jump

kangaroo

key

kick

kite

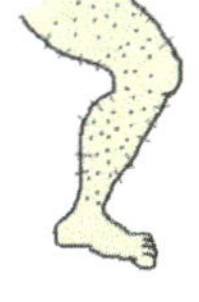
leg

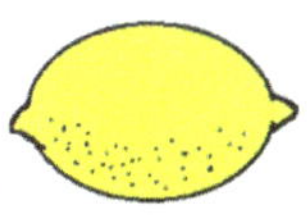
lemon

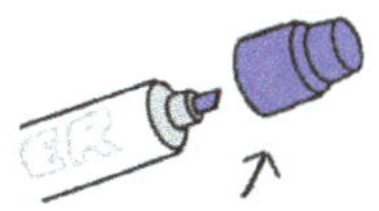
lid

lion

Word List

Unit 5

milk

monkey

moon

mouse

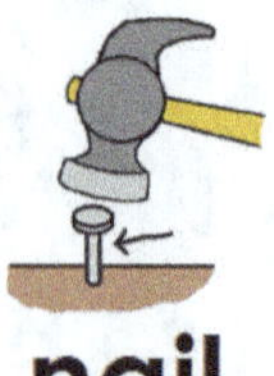
nail

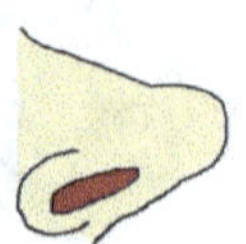
nose

nurse

nut

octopus

old

ostrich

ox

Unit 6

pants

peach

poop

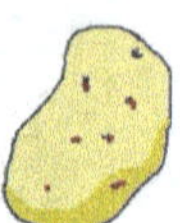
potato

queen

question

quick

quiet

radio

red

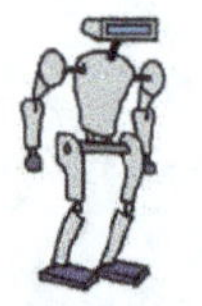
robot

run

Word List

Unit 7

 sad	 sit	 smell	 sun
tear	 ten	tiger	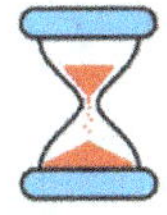 time
umbrella	umpire	 under	 up
van	vest	 violin	 vomit

Unit 8

 water	 wave	 window	 wish
box	fix	fox	 six
yawn	yellow	young	 yo-yo
zebra	 zero	zipper	zoo 

What's this page here for?

Well, those flashcards had
to start on a odd page, and
we had no content for this
page.

a / an

and

all

on

in

the

OUR SIGHT WORD FLASH CARDS! 

no	**lift**
like	**get**
oh	**not**

did

you

your

has

put

one

OUR SIGHT WORD FLASH CARDS!

by	**fellow**
say	**go**
to	**win**

OUR SIGHT WORD FLASH CARDS!

I	had
it	wait

Phonics Series

Preschool:

Kindergarten:

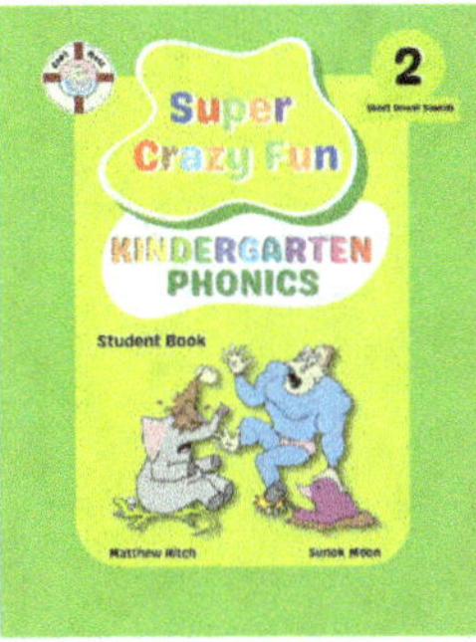

Elementary School Junior:

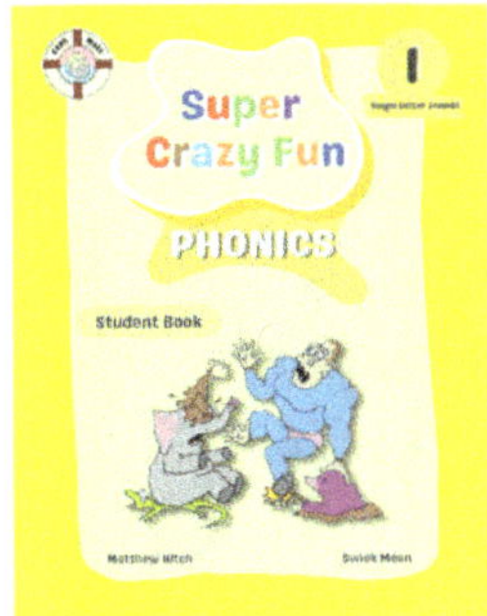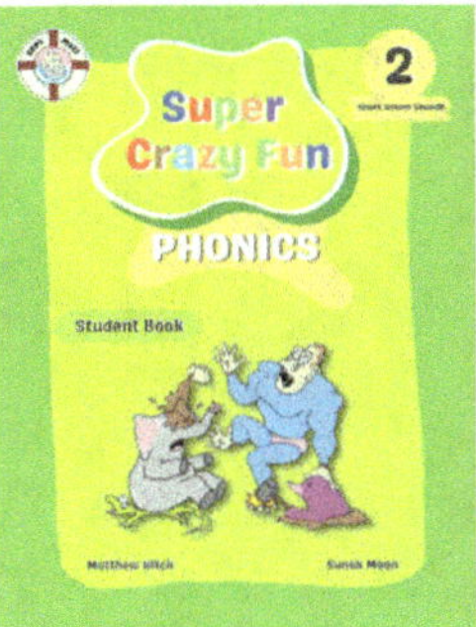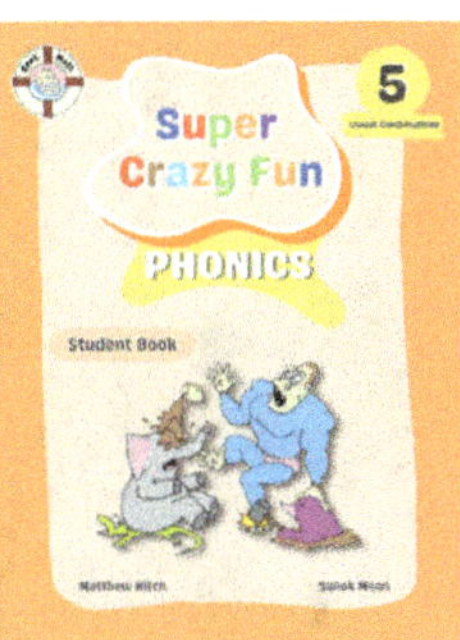

Elementary School Senior/Remedial:

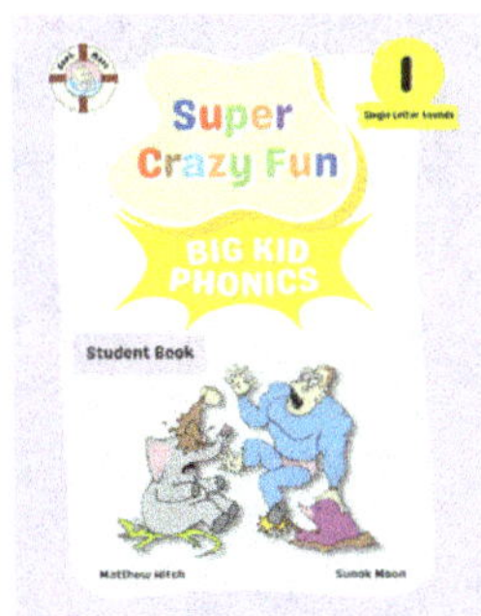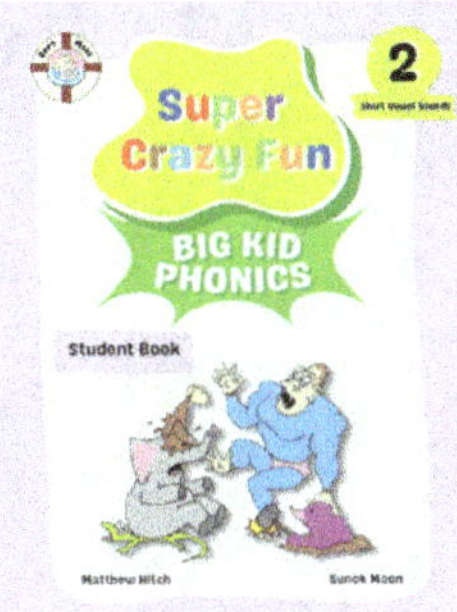

www.ingramcontent.com/pod-product-compliance
Lightning Source LLC
Chambersburg PA
CBHW081317150726
48001CB00020B/2736